COFFEE WITH MY DEMONS PART 2

Coffee With My Demons Part 2

The Past- Special Edition

DR. ALEC LARACUENTE

Vitalis CM

CONTENTS

PREFACE

Welcome to the second volume of "Coffee with My Demons Part 2: Healing the Past." If you've already taken the first steps toward understanding your inner demons and embracing vulnerability, self-compassion, and resilience, you're ready to delve even deeper into your journey. The lessons from the first volume are the foundation for what's to come. It's time to explore the shadows of your past and use holistic tools to reclaim your life from unresolved traumas, limiting beliefs, and nonadaptive behaviors. This journey requires courage and strength. Facing your shadows means peeling back the layers and confronting the uncomfortable. But remember, you have the power to heal and grow. Soul retrieving and holistic exploration of your past can be challenging and illuminating. It's an opportunity to liberate yourself from the weight of past traumas and emerge with a profound sense of understanding, forgiveness, and empowerment. As you progress, remember to carry the tools and insights you've gained—approach this journey with openness, self-compassion, and the understanding that taking your time is okay. We'll work together to release the shackles of the past and reframe your narrative, enabling you to step into the future with renewed purpose, resilience, and clarity. Through this transformative expedition, know that you're not alone. Dr. Alec is here with you, navigating the challenges and celebrating the victories together. You've already demonstrated incredible courage by stepping into this path. Now, it's time to move forward with hope, determination, and a shared commitment to becoming the best versions of ourselves. Thank you for entrusting me with this vital part of your life.

Let's continue this journey with gratitude and anticipation, paving the way for a future of profound healing and growth.

With gratitude and anticipation,
Dr. Alec Laracuente

COPYRIGHT

ISBN: 979-8-9889666-6-1 (Paperback Version English)

Front cover image Artist: A. Ivar, Ph.D.

Book design: A. Ivar Ph.D.

First printing edition 2023.

www.coffeewithmydemons.com

coffeewithmydemons@gmail.com

DEDICATORY

Dear Ancestors, I acknowledge your enduring presence and the profound impact you have had on my life. Your stories, struggles, and triumphs have shaped the contours of my existence in subtle and profound ways.

With gratitude and reverence, I honor your legacy and hold space for your pain to be heard and acknowledged. Your journeys, marked by resilience and heartache, have left imprints upon my soul that continue to guide me as I navigate my healing. To those who bore the weight of generational trauma, I stand on your shoulders, entrusted with healing what was left unhealed.

In the crucible of your struggles, I find the strength to confront my shadows and to release what no longer serves. And to the guardians of resilience, I offer my deepest gratitude for creating the space for healing to unfurl its wings. Through these words, I strive to honor your memory, bring to light the silenced stories, and pave a path toward healing for us all.

May they serve as a bridge between worlds, an offering of healing, and a tribute to the unbroken thread of love that weaves us all together.

With boundless gratitude and reverence,
Dr. Alec...

COFFEE WITH MY DEMONS PART 1 SUMMARY

While informative and insightful, this summary should be viewed as a companion rather than a replacement for reading the first book. Its purpose is to serve as a refresher or to present the previous information in a more colloquial and condensed form.

Reading the first book provides a comprehensive and in-depth exploration of the topics discussed, offering a richer understanding of the concepts, strategies, and insights shared by the author. It allows readers to immerse themselves fully in the transformative journey towards inner peace and self-discovery.

This summary, however, acts as a handy reference, reminding readers of the key takeaways and guiding principles from the first book. It condenses the material into a more digestible format, making revisiting and reinforcing the crucial messages easier. It's beneficial for those who have already read the first book and want a quick recap or need a simplified version of the content.

In essence, the summary complements the first book by providing a different perspective and accessibility to the information it contains. However, reading the first book remains essential for the full depth and breadth of the author's insights.

If you want to go straight to book two, please go to page #57

INTRODUCTION

Greetings, and welcome to the revised short edition of "Coffee with My Demons." As a pain management doctor, I have witnessed firsthand how mental struggles can impact my patients and encountered my inner demons. This is a condensed version of the original, designed to serve as an introduction in case you still need to read the first edition.

I understand the challenges of dealing with these issues, so I wrote this book. It differs from other self-help books as we will only delve deep into some mental demon now. Instead, we will focus on providing you with mental clarity and strength for what lies ahead.

Consider this summary book as a starting point, where you will receive the tools necessary for self-discovery. In subsequent volumes, we will explore your past, assist you in healing, and liberate you from generational trauma.

This first volume is intended to help you develop a strong mind. You will learn about self-compassion, mindfulness, setting boundaries, and self-care – all essential for a satisfying life. Our goal is to help you create lasting change and personal freedom. This strength will prepare you for more profound self-discovery in the next volume.

Ultimately, we'll empower you to break free from generational trauma and focus on a resilient, emotionally healthy future. "Coffee with My Demons" is more than a book; it's your guide to a trans-formative journey. I hope it brings you peace and freedom.

SUMMARY CHAPTER 1

Imagine your mind like a house where you spend most of your time. This house has many rooms, each holding different thoughts and feelings. Some rooms are bright with good memories, while others hide in shadows, containing mental blocks and unwanted behaviors.

These "demons" are like old stuff in your house, including traumas, anxieties, and habits. They're memories and emotions you haven't fully processed, just taking up space in your mind.

As you go through life, you live with these demons. Some you're used to, even if they're not helpful. Others you've locked away because they hurt too much. But forgotten monsters are also hiding in your mind without you realizing it.

Your mind-house needs care, like your real home. Bright rooms need nurturing, while demon-filled ones need cleaning. But facing these darker parts can be challenging.
Start by acknowledging your demons; this is the first step to healing. This book will guide you through cleaning and organizing your mental house, respecting your readiness to face certain demons.

Remember, you're not alone. We'll explore your mind together, shedding light on forgotten corners. As you understand your mental demons, you'll gain the strength to control your mental house.

How? By changing behaviors and thoughts, using the book's knowledge and activities as your cleaning tools. You'll find various activities and writing spaces here to help you clean your house and eventually have "coffee" with your mental demons, saying goodbye to them.

Activity 1.0: Inner and Outer House. Harmony.

1. **Morning Ritual:** *Start the day positively. Greet the day smiling, even if you have a noisy alarm clock. Begin with love and positivity.*
2. **Tending to the Sanctuary:** *Clean your physical space and reflect on decluttering your mind. Each item has a place, just like each thought.*
3. **Mindful Meal Preparation:** *Prepare meals mindfully. Appreciate the nourishment. Even if it's just cereal, serve it with mindfulness.*
4. **The Art of Cleaning:** *Treat cleaning as meditation. Imagine it washes away negative energy from your mental space. This goes for laundry and everything else.*
5. **Cozy Corners of Comfort:** *Create cozy spots in your living space. Fill them with things that bring joy, like positive experiences for your mind.*
6. **Restful Repose:** *Make your bedroom a sanctuary of comfort. Follow sleep hygiene techniques for a peaceful slumber.*
7. **Reflective Reading Nook:** *Designate a space for reading and reflection. Engage with books that strengthen you for your inner battles.*
8. **Mindful Cleaning Up** *End the day with gratitude for joyful moments and compassion for challenges. Clean up thoughtfully, like cleansing your mind before sleep.*

These simple activities echo the mental space we want: tidy, tranquil, and nourishing. You inspire clarity and contentment by caring for your physical and mental spaces. Virginia Woolf reminds us that our psychological and physical spaces are connected, and by tending to both, we can genuinely think, love, and live well.

Section 1: Side effects of transformation.

As we start our journey to mental well-being, let's think about our "mind house." We'll do an exercise to understand it better and identify our inner struggles later. Get ready to clean your inner house and remove those struggles.

Now, let's talk about what happens when we transform ourselves. The changes are expected. Prepare for laughter and tears, saying goodbye to old habits, moments of clarity, and strong connections. Your life will feel magical and have a new sense of purpose. Don't fear these changes; instead, welcome them with open arms. They'll help you lead an extraordinary life.

This book is for everyone, including the younger generation. They've taught me that clear, concise lists make understanding easier. So, you'll see lists often in this book to help you understand better.

Side effects of the transformative Odyssey:

1. Positivity Shines: When you work on your mental and emotional health, you'll glow with positivity. People might wonder how you stay so happy. Good vibes can rub off on others; some may want to know your secret.
2. Drama Takes a Backseat: Those who love drama might find it doesn't work around you anymore. Your inner peace can stop conflicts from becoming a big deal. It might surprise drama lovers when they see you're not as interested in their theatrics.
3. Empathy Grows: Your heart will strengthen as you explore your emotions. Friends might come to you for advice and a listening ear. Being empathetic is a big responsibility but also a chance for meaningful connections.
4. Setting Boundaries: You'll learn to set healthy boundaries. This might surprise people who are used to pushing your limits. They'll eventually admire your newfound assertiveness.
5. Resilience Builds: Life's challenges will still come, but you'll handle them better. Your strength might surprise those who once doubted you.
6. Goodbye Toxic Relationships: While improving yourself, you'll notice toxic relationships. It's okay to let them go. New, better connections will come your way.
7. Your Life, Your Story: You'll control your thoughts and emotions more. Life becomes an exciting adventure; you're the hero shaping your destiny.
8. Unleash Creativity: Your creativity will burst forth. You might feel like writing, dancing, painting, or doing something artistic. Let your creativity flow and shape your world.

As you work on your mental well-being, you'll experience these "side effects" that can be surprisingly impactful and even amusing. It's all part of the journey to a healthier mind and soul.

CHAPTER 2 SUMMARY: VULNERABILITY

Vulnerability is being brave with your feelings, thoughts, and fears, even if it feels scary. It's like taking off a mask and showing who you are. It's not a sign of weakness; it takes a lot of strength.

Here are some essential things about vulnerability:

1. **Being Brave: It takes courage to show your true self, even if you're afraid others might not like it. It's like standing on the edge of a cliff, not knowing what will happen next.**
2. **Sharing with the Right People: Vulnerability isn't about telling everyone everything. It's about sharing with the people you trust and care about you.**
3. **It's Not Just About Problems: Vulnerability isn't only about sharing when things are bad. It's also about sharing when things are good, like when you're happy or excited.**
4. **It's Safe with the Right People: It's natural to worry that people might use your feelings against you. But if you choose the right people to share with, it's usually safe.**
5. **It's Not a One-Time Thing: You don't just do it once and you're done. It's an ongoing thing, like a journey of getting to know yourself and others better.**

Vulnerability is a way to connect with others, grow as a person, and become more resilient. It's not something to fear; it's something to embrace for a better and more fulfilling life.

Section II: Healing the Mental House through Vulnerability.

When we're kind to ourselves and open about our feelings, it's like creating a powerful team. Self-compassion means treating ourselves like we would a good friend - being understanding and gentle with ourselves. Vulnerability is when we dare to show our true selves, even if it means sharing our fears and imperfections.

When we're open and vulnerable, we realize that everyone goes through tough times - we're not alone. This understanding helps us treat ourselves kindly, knowing it's okay to be imperfect. When we drop the act of perfection, self-compassion grows, and we start healing and growing.

But it's not just about us; it's also about others. When we're open, we connect with people better, and we can understand their struggles. Vulnerability lets others feel safe around us, and they can share their challenges, too. This compassion not only helps us but also our relationships and communities.

In therapy and personal relationships, trust and connection are super important. Vulnerability helps here, too. Being open and empathetic in treatment creates a safe space for people to share their problems. In personal relationships, sharing our fears and past issues brings us closer. It takes courage, but it deepens our bonds.

Also, it's easier to resolve conflicts when we're open about our feelings. By sharing our fears and needs, we understand each other better. Vulnerability builds bridges for understanding and trust.

So, in therapy and with loved ones, vulnerability is critical. It helps create empathy, acceptance, and intense bonds. This leads to deep healing and better, more meaningful relationships. Openness helps us connect, grow, and heal together.

Section 3: Discernment.

Discernment is like having a superpower that helps us make intelligent choices and see things. The thing inside us guides us to make good decisions and tell right from wrong. It's crucial for avoiding quick, impulsive choices and bad judgments.

To get good at discernment, we need to know ourselves. That means understanding our own biases, fears, and wants. When we see why we make choices, we can make better ones. We must also stay in the moment and know what's happening. That way, we can think clearly and not just react.

Listening to different points of view and learning new things is also essential. When we talk to others and read different ideas, we get smarter. We should be open-minded and consider many sides of a situation.

Lastly, we should learn from our mistakes. Instead of feeling wrong about them, we can use them to improve. This helps us make more intelligent choices in the future.

When we're good at discernment, life gets less confusing. We make choices that fit our beliefs and where we want to go. It helps us have a more meaningful life. With discernment, we can take on the "Coffee with My Demons" journey with wisdom and get the most out of it.

Activity 2.1: Vulnerability Writing.

Step 1: Get Comfortable. Find a quiet, cozy place where you won't be bothered. Bring a pen and some paper. You might also want soft music or gentle lighting to make it a soothing space.

Step 2: Think About Your Feelings. Start by taking some deep breaths to calm yourself. Think about your feelings and what's been on your mind lately. It's okay to be honest, even if your feelings are challenging.

Step 3: Pick a Vulnerability Question. Choose one of the questions that feels right for you. For example:

- *Tell about a time when you felt vulnerable and how it affected you.*
- *Write about something you're afraid of or not confident about and how it's affecting your life.*
- *Describe when you had trouble showing your feelings and what you learned from it.*

Step 4: Write Honestly. Now, start writing your thoughts in response to the question. Be kind to yourself, and don't worry about making it perfect. This is a place to be accurate and write from your heart.

Step 5: Face Uncomfortable Feelings. While you write, you might feel uncomfortable or vulnerable. That's okay; it's part of the process. Remember that being open like this is a brave way to be kind to yourself. It helps you grow and heal.

Step 6: Think About What You Wrote. After you're done writing, take a moment to think about what you wrote. See if you notice any patterns or things that come up a lot. Think about how this writing exercise has changed how you see your feelings and experiences.

Step 7: Share If You Want (Only in a safe group). If you feel okay, you can share your writing with a trusted friend or a small group. This can make you feel more connected and help others understand you better. But remember, you can share if you want to.

Step 8: Keep Doing It. Make this writing a regular thing to improve at being open and vulnerable. You can do it weekly or whenever you need to explore your feelings. With time, you'll learn more about yourself and better handle your emotions.

Vulnerability is a brave way to learn more about yourself and grow. This writing activity creates a safe space to be honest and connect better with your emotions.

CHAPTER 3 SUMMARY:
SELF-COMPASSION.

Self-compassion and forgiveness are special tools for tidying up our feelings and thoughts, just like cleaning a messy room. They help make our minds and hearts cleaner and more welcoming for healing and growing.

Self-compassion means being friendly to ourselves, especially when things are tough or we make mistakes. Instead of being mean to ourselves, we learn to accept our flaws with kindness. It's like getting rid of the dust of self-criticism and talking to ourselves kindlier.

Forgiveness is like a robust cleaning solution for our hearts and minds. It helps us let go of old hurts, grudges, and bad feelings from the past. By forgiving ourselves and others, we clear away the heavy baggage we've carried for a long time. It's like opening windows in our minds, letting in fresh air and light.

When we practice self-compassion and forgiveness, we become the boss of our inner world. Instead of being controlled by old feelings and problems, we learn to deal with them with kindness and understanding. Self-compassion helps us overcome self-doubt and insecurities, while forgiveness helps us mop up old grudges and hurt.

But remember, practicing self-compassion and forgiveness doesn't mean we become perfect inside. It means we accept that we're not perfect, and that's okay.

These practices help us build a strong foundation for feeling good and understanding ourselves better. We become better at handling our feelings and thoughts, even when new challenges arise. Through self-compassion and forgiveness, we become stronger and kinder to ourselves, like caring for a special place with love and grace.

Section 1: How to achieve self-compassion.

Acknowledging the Need for Self-Compassion: Recognizing the importance of self-compassion is the first step in improving your mental and emotional well-being. Often, we are very hard on ourselves, constantly criticizing ourselves for our mistakes or perceived flaws. This self-critical attitude creates a hostile environment in our minds, making it difficult to deal with emotional issues and grow.

Self-compassion means treating ourselves with kindness, understanding, and acceptance. It's about acknowledging that we're human and, like everyone else, face challenges and make mistakes. Instead of being overly critical, self-compassion encourages us to be kinder to ourselves, which helps us clear away negative self-talk and self-blame. This creates a more positive and nurturing mental space.

When we practice self-compassion, it's like opening the windows of our minds to let in fresh air and light. It frees us from the weight of past regrets and emotional baggage, making room for personal growth and renewal. Self-compassion also helps us become more self-aware and confident as we learn to find contentment within ourselves rather than seeking external validation.

Daily Self-Compassion Practice: Daily self-compassion practice is a powerful way to improve your emotional well-being and strengthen your connection with yourself. This practice involves setting aside time each day for self-reflection and self-kindness.

During this daily practice, you create a quiet and peaceful space to center yourself and turn your focus inward. Deep breaths help you ground yourself in the present moment, bringing a sense of calm and clarity. You then acknowledge your emotions and experiences without judgment, even the uncomfortable ones. Instead of pushing away negative feelings, you treat them with tenderness, recognizing that they are a natural part of being human.

This daily practice helps you develop a compassionate inner dialogue. You become more aware of your self-talk, replacing self-critical thoughts with kind and encouraging words. Instead of beating yourself up over mistakes, you offer yourself comfort and understanding. This compassionate inner voice acts like a broom, sweeping away self-doubt and self-blame, creating a nurturing space for emotional growth and self-acceptance.

By engaging in daily self-compassion practice, you infuse self-care and self-love into your life. It is a guiding light, illuminating your growth and healing path. This practice empowers you to be gentle with yourself, embrace your vulnerabilities, and find strength in your imperfections. Over time, it deepens your connection with yourself, making you more attuned to your needs and emotions. This daily ritual becomes a beacon of compassion, leading you on a profound journey of self-discovery and inner transformation.

Activity 3.1 Self Compassion.

Daily Self-Compassion Practice: *To practice self-compassion daily, set aside some quiet time in a comfortable space. Take deep breaths and repeat compassionate statements like "I deserve love and kindness," "I forgive myself for mistakes," or "I embrace my emotions without judgment." These affirmations help cultivate self-compassion. You can choose the ones that resonate most with you. Doing this regularly helps nurture a compassionate mindset and improves emotional well-being.*

Embrace Imperfections with Kindness: *Accepting your imperfections with kindness is a powerful practice. In a world that often values perfection, it's essential to understand that nobody is perfect. Treat yourself kindly instead of criticizing yourself for your flaws, just as you would a dear friend. Also, recognize that making mistakes is a part of being human and an opportunity for growth. Practicing this for yourself will make it easier to empathize and understand others' imperfections.*

Cultivate Self-Compassionate Self-Talk: *Transform your inner dialogue by speaking to yourself with kindness, especially during tough times or after making mistakes. Pay attention to your self-talk and replace self-critical thoughts with compassionate words. Instead of beating yourself up for errors, offer yourself comfort and understanding. This shift in self-talk acts like a broom, sweeping away self-doubt and negativity and creating a nurturing space for growth and healing. It helps you become your ally and advocate, recognizing that mistakes are learning opportunities and nobody is perfect.*

These practices shape your inner world, fostering self-acceptance, emotional well-being, and resilience. You build a foundation of self-love and self-empowerment by speaking to yourself with kindness and understanding.

Activity 3.2: Changing Negative Self-Talk to Self-Compassionate Self-Talk.

In this activity, you are given scenarios with negative self-talk and are encouraged to change them into self-compassionate self-talk. This helps you identify and change repetitive negative thoughts in your mind. Here are the scenarios and their reframed versions:

Negative Self-Talk: "I'm such a failure. I can't believe I messed up again. I'll never get it right." Self-Compassionate Self-Talk: "Making mistakes is a part of being human. It's okay to stumble sometimes. I can learn from this experience and use it as an opportunity to grow and improve."

Negative Self-Talk: "I'm so stupid for not understanding this. I'll never be good enough." Self-Compassionate Self-Talk: "It's normal to find certain things challenging. I am capable of learning and growing. I will be patient with myself and seek support if needed."

Negative Self-Talk: "Nobody likes me. I'm unlikeable and unworthy of love and friendship." Self-Compassionate Self-Talk: "Feeling disconnected from others is a common human experience. I am worthy of love and belonging, just as I am. I can take steps to nurture and build meaningful connections."

Negative Self-Talk: "I'll never be as successful as others. I'm a failure compared to them." Self-Compassionate Self-Talk: "Comparing myself to others doesn't serve me. Each person's journey is unique, and I am on my path. I celebrate my achievements and focus on my personal growth and progress."

Negative Self-Talk: "I can't believe I let everyone down. I'm so useless." Self-Compassionate Self-Talk: "Feeling overwhelmed and unable to meet everyone's expectations is normal. I am not perfect, and that's okay. I'll communicate my limits and focus on doing my best."

Negative Self-Talk: "I'm so awkward and weird. No one wants to be around me." Self-Compassionate Self-Talk: "I have unique qualities that make me who I am. It's okay to be different. I accept myself and appreciate my individuality."

Negative Self-Talk: "I should have known better. I'm so naive." Self-Compassionate Self-Talk: "Hindsight is a valuable teacher. I am allowed to make mistakes and learn from them. I will be kind to myself and use this experience to make wiser decisions in the future."

Negative Self-Talk: "I'm so weak for feeling this way. I should be stronger." Self-Compassionate Self-Talk: "Feeling vulnerable is a part of being human. I can be gentle with myself and acknowledge my emotions without judgment. My feelings are valid, and I will give myself the space and time to process them."

In each scenario, you're encouraged to replace self-criticism with self-compassion by being understanding, kind, and accepting of yourself. This practice helps you let go of self-criticism, creating a space for personal growth, healing, and self-acceptance.

Personal Note: As you start your journey to be kinder to yourself and clean up your inner thoughts and feelings, know that it won't always be easy. There might be times when you face difficulties and setbacks. Remember to be patient with yourself during those moments and value every step you take.

The strength you gain from being compassionate to yourself will help you confront your inner struggles with bravery, empathy, and understanding. When you embrace your vulnerabilities and accept them, it will help you create stronger connections with yourself and the people around you.

Think of your inner journey, like conversing over coffee with your internal struggles (your "demons"). This dialogue can transform you as you face and heal from past emotional wounds. It will bring you a sense of liberation and empowerment.

Imagine self-compassion as a broom that sweeps away self-doubt and negative thoughts, making space for personal growth, resilience, and deep inner peace. Remember that your past does not define you as you sip your coffee with your internal struggles. Instead, you're limited by the strength of your self-compassion and the love you show to yourself and the world.

CHAPTER 4 SUMMARY: FORGIVENESS.

Forgiveness is like a deep emotional cleansing. Just as dust collects in hidden corners of our homes, emotional pain, and old grudges gather in the corners of our hearts and minds. When we choose to forgive, it's like using a powerful mop to wash away those old hurts and grudges that have been with us for too long. This freeing act creates space inside us for healing and renewal.

Through forgiveness, we regain control of our emotions and thoughts. Instead of being weighed down by anger and Resentment, we become the designers of our emotional world, shaping it with kindness and understanding. As designers, we understand that while there might still be some emotional baggage and painful memories, forgiveness guides us toward self-empowerment. It's not about forgetting the past but changing how we relate to the pain and letting it go.

Forgiveness gives us the freedom to rewrite our inner story and to choose the emotions we want to feel. We no longer see ourselves only through the lens of past hurts or what others have done to us. Instead, we view our inner world as a constantly changing canvas, influenced by our compassion and self-acceptance. This new control allows us to explore the different aspects of our mind and heart with bravery, knowing we have the strength to face any lingering pain.

Even if some parts of our inner world need more attention, forgiveness gives us the wisdom to deal with these areas gracefully and kindly. We understand that we're a work in progress, and that's fine. Forgiveness helps us tackle future challenges with a sense of inner peace, knowing that we are not defined by our past mistakes or the pain we've been through.

So, forgiveness is like a mop that cleans our inner world, freeing us from the weight of old resentments and emotional baggage. When we embrace forgiveness, we become the masters of our dynamic world, capable of facing our inner demons with bravery and kindness. By accepting forgiveness, we liberate ourselves from the past and open ourselves up to a journey of healing and growth. Remember, forgiveness doesn't erase history; it shapes our present and future with warmth and understanding. Through forgiveness, we discover empowerment, resilience, and deep self-love, allowing us to become the architects of our inner world and the authors of our transformative journey.

Section 1: How to cultivate forgiveness.

Step 1: Recognize Resentment is like a heavy burden from past hurts. To deal with it, first, we must admit it's there. This can be hard because it means facing the pain it brings. But by acknowledging it, we start the process of healing.

Step 2: Think About Unforgiveness Consider how holding onto grudges affects you and your relationships. Forgiveness is like letting go of a heavy weight and making room for healing.

Step 3: Be Kind and Understand Others. Empathy means caring about others' feelings. Start by being kind to yourself and understanding your emotions. This sets the stage for being kind to others.

Listen without judgment when others talk. Learn about different people and cultures. When there's a conflict, try to see things from their perspective. Practicing empathy makes your relationships stronger and helps you feel better inside.

Step 4: Let Go of Revenge only keeps us in pain. Instead, try to understand why someone hurt you. Replace revenge thoughts with kind ones. This helps you find inner peace.

Step 5: Be Kind to Yourself. Treat yourself with kindness, like you would to someone you love. Watch how you talk to yourself. Accept that nobody's perfect. Embrace your uniqueness, especially when you make mistakes. Set healthy boundaries and take care of yourself. Self-compassion is a journey of self-discovery and growth.

Step 6: Do Forgiveness Rituals Include forgiveness practices in your daily life? Write forgiveness letters (even if you don't send them), meditate on forgiveness, or do forgiveness exercises. These rituals help you let go of past hurt and make room for healing.

In short, these steps help you let go of revenge, be kind to yourself, and practice forgiveness rituals to find inner peace and growth.

Activity 4.2 Liberating Resentment.

Find a quiet and comfortable place. Grab a pen and a journal. Close your eyes and take deep breaths. Think about past events that hurt or upset you. Open your eyes and write about these events honestly. Describe how they made you feel. Be kind to yourself and know it's normal to feel this way. Read what you wrote and look for patterns in your feelings. This helps you understand why you think this way. Closing your journal, remind yourself that acknowledging these feelings is a brave step towards healing. Be patient with yourself. This activity helps you start the process of finding inner peace.

CHAPTER 5 SUMMARY:
CULTIVATING RESILIENCE.

Chapter 5 of "Coffee with My Demons" explores the importance of resilience in facing life's challenges. Resilience is a skill that can be developed and strengthened through evidence-based strategies:

1. **Positive Reframing:** This involves shifting your perspective to focus on growth and learning opportunities in difficult situations. It helps you see obstacles as stepping stones for personal development.
2. **Building a Support System:** Just as a house needs a strong structure, you need supportive relationships to help you through tough times. Having caring and understanding people around you provides comfort and encouragement.
3. **Mindfulness** means paying attention to your thoughts and emotions without judgment. It helps you respond to challenges with clarity and calmness.
4. **Self-Compassion:** Self-compassion involves treating yourself with kindness and acceptance. It gives you the strength to persevere and find inner peace during challenging moments.
5. **Embracing a Growth Mindset:** Instead of seeing setbacks and failures as defeats, view them as opportunities for growth and self-discovery. A growth mindset helps you overcome obstacles with determination.

Cultivating resilience is about developing the tools to bounce back and thrive despite life's difficulties. It's not about avoiding challenges but becoming more robust and wiser as you face them. By practicing resilience, you can confront life's challenges with unwavering strength and emerge more resilient than ever.

Activity 5: Cultivating Resilience.

To cultivate resilience, find a quiet space with a journal and pen. Follow these steps:

1. **Recall Past Challenges:** *Write down three challenging situations or setbacks you've faced. Remember the emotions and thoughts you experienced.*
2. **Find Positive Outcomes:** *Next to each challenge, note at least one positive outcome or lesson from the experience. Reflect on your growth and strengths developed during those times.*
3. **Identify Inner Strengths:** *Identify three inner strengths that helped you overcome these challenges. These could be qualities like perseverance, courage, adaptability, or compassion.*
4. **Apply Strengths to Future Challenges:** *Imagine facing a potential future challenge. Write down how you can use these inner strengths to navigate it. Visualize yourself confidently and determinedly overcoming it.*

This activity helps you recognize your inner power and build a resilient mindset. Just as a substantial house is built brick by brick, resilience is cultivated step by step. Stability is about equipping yourself to face difficulties with grace and strength. You are the architect of your resilience, and with each challenge, you become stronger and more resilient in the face of life's challenges.

Personal Note: Resilience empowers us to rise with grace in life's storms. We nurture resilience with courage, compassion, and growth like a conductor. It's our compass through life's challenges, reminding us of our power. Cultivating resilience, we become composers of our symphony, harmonizing challenges and triumphs into a masterpiece of strength, wisdom, and unwavering spirit.

CHAPTER 6 SUMMARY: NURTURING A GROWTH MINDSET - UNLOCKING THE PATH TO TRIUMPH.

Nurturing a growth mindset is like a guiding light in our inner house. It helps us clean our inner world, improve our lives, and conquer our inner demons. As a seed grows in fertile soil, a growth mindset lets us develop our skills through dedication, effort, and resilience. This chapter explores how a growth mindset helps us face challenges, see failures as opportunities, and push past our limits to achieve greatness.

Section 1: Embracing the Growth Mindset.

Embracing a growth mindset is like making a lifelong friend who helps us grow and discover ourselves. We nurture this mindset within us, much like a gardener cares for seeds so that they can become a powerful force of change.

To embrace the growth mindset:

1. **Curiosity and Openness**: Instead of seeing challenges and failures as setbacks, we see them as opportunities to learn and improve. It's like trimming a plant to help it grow better.
2. **Positive Language**: We replace negative thoughts with affirmations of growth and improvement. This positive outlook is like nurturing a garden for change.

3. **Self-Compassion**: We're kind to ourselves when facing set-backs because we understand they're part of learning. It's like gentle rain during a drought, helping us grow even when things are tough.
4. **Community or Independence**: Surrounding ourselves with like-minded people who support growth is beneficial. But it's also okay to be independent, like a strong tree protecting its surroundings.

Embracing the growth mindset transforms our inner world and improves our lives. It helps us face challenges with grace and resilience, becoming the architects of our growth and self-discovery.

Section 2: Navigating the Terrain of Challenges.

Navigating life's challenges is like embarking on an exciting journey. Imagine you're an adventurer venturing into uncharted territories. These challenges aren't roadblocks; they're more like opportunities for learning and self-improvement. So, how do we navigate these challenges?

First, think of yourself as an adaptable captain steering a ship. As a skilled sailor adjusts to changing tides, you must stay flexible when life throws curveballs. This flexibility is your strength, helping you weather the storms with grace and determination.

Next, consider challenges as canvases for painting your life story. Talented artists find beauty in every brushstroke, even in mistakes. Similarly, viewing setbacks as valuable lessons transforms obstacles into stepping stones for growth.

Mindfulness is your anchor during this journey. Like a ship anchored steadily in choppy waters, mindfulness keeps you grounded in the present. It lets you stay calm and collected when facing challenges. Being aware of your thoughts and emotions helps you make better choices.

And remember, you don't have to go it alone. Think of yourself as part of a caravan crossing vast deserts. Just as fellow travelers offer encouragement, empathy, and different perspectives, having a support system can make your journey through challenges less daunting.

This journey through challenges transforms you. It's like becoming a seasoned explorer who believes that challenges are opportunities for growth and self-discovery. With a positive mindset, you become the captain of your ship, navigating challenges with courage and curiosity. In the vast landscape of challenges, you'll discover your true potential and become more resilient than ever imagined.

Section 3: Expanding Beyond Limitations.

Life is a journey filled with challenges, ups, and downs. These experiences shape who we are. But sometimes, we create our limits because of self-doubt, fear, or think we can't change.

But the good news is, we can break free from these limits. We have the power to discover our full potential.

To do this, we need to start by believing in possibilities. Instead of seeing problems as roadblocks, see them as chances to learn and row. Life is constantly changing, and every experience is a chance to improve.

Courage is key. We need to be brave and try new things, even scary ones. Like a bird learning to fly, we must leave our comfort zone to grow.

Inside us, there's strength and belief. We can overcome obstacles and limits. When things go wrong, we should see them as lessons. Determination pushes us forward.

On this journey, we need supportive friends or mentors. Like a garden needs care, we need people who believe in us. But even if you don't have them, remember, you're not alone. We're here with you.

Breaking limits is like discovering your true self. It's about being bold, believing in yourself, and not giving up. Your potential is vast, and you can do amazing things. So, take this journey with an open heart and a solid commitment to growth. The possibilities are endless.

Personal Note: Remember that growing and expanding is a life-long journey. It's not something you reach and stop; it's a continuous process of discovering yourself and becoming more assertive. Learning is like the wind that pushes you forward.

Be brave and strong, like wings that carry you beyond your limits. And remember to be kind to yourself. Growth takes time, and every step is a victory, no matter how small.

Your mind is like a garden; every possibility is a seed waiting to bloom. You have the power to shape your life. Remember this, and you'll be the architect of your transformation.

Activity 6.1: Seed of Growth

Find a quiet, comfy place with no distractions. Take a few deep breaths to relax.

Now, write in your journal. First, jot down three recent challenges or ones you expect in the future.

Think about how you felt when these challenges came up. Did you doubt yourself or feel anxious? Maybe you got overwhelmed or discouraged.

Now, try this: change how you see these challenges. Write a positive and powerful way to think about each one. For example, if you are worried about a presentation, see it as a chance to improve public speaking and show your expertise.

Picture yourself excited and curious about these challenges, not scared. Imagine you're going to beat them with determination and strength.

While thinking about this, write down three things you can do to deal with each challenge. Make them small steps so they're easy enough.

Celebrate that you're ready to have a growth mindset and face challenges head-on. Remember, every challenge helps you learn and grow.

Come back to this next time you feel unsure or face a new challenge. Read your new positive thoughts and your plan. This will help you believe in yourself and your ability to exceed limits.

Doing this activity helps you grow a growth mindset inside you. It means you start seeing challenges as chances to grow and change, and you look at things more positively. Your growth mindset will strengthen as you keep thinking this way and staying curious and determined. It'll guide you to many unique possibilities on your journey to discovering and becoming your best self.

CHAPTER 7 SUMMARY: EMBRACING THE PRESENT MOMENT - MINDFULNESS AND MEDITATION.

In our busy lives, stress and distractions often take over. Mindfulness is like a calm anchor that helps us focus on the here and now. It's about fully understanding our thoughts, feelings, and sensations. This can help clear our minds and bring us inner peace. These mindfulness tools can help in your daily life and cleaning your inner house.

Mindfulness is about being present in the moment. It's like slowing down time and quieting the noise in our heads. With mindfulness, we watch our thoughts and feelings without judging them, like a kind observer watching the ups and downs of life.

When we practice mindfulness, we learn to accept things as they are. We stop fighting and start going with the flow of life. This helps us forget the past and stop worrying about the future. We find peace in simply being.

Mindfulness is also a way to discover who we are and treat ourselves with kindness. It's like peeling away the distractions to find our true selves. Mindfulness reminds us that we're not just our thoughts or what's happening around us; we're the ones watching it all.

With mindfulness, we tune in to life's music, where each moment has its memorable tune. We savor every bit of now, like enjoying a rare treat. Mindfulness shows us that life's treasure is the journey, not just the destination.

Mindfulness is an invitation to enjoy the beauty of the present moment. It's like a journey within ourselves, where we find peace, self-acceptance, and a deep connection to life. Try mindfulness with an open heart and a curious mind, and you'll discover the simple, serene beauty inside you.

Activity 7.1 Meditation Exercises for Present-Moment Awareness:

You can do simple meditation exercises to practice mindfulness and cultivate its essence. Find a quiet and comfy spot, sit in a relaxed position, and gently close your eyes.

1. ***Breath Awareness:*** *Pay attention to your breath. Feel your chest rise and fall, or notice the air flowing through your nose. If your mind drifts away, gently bring your focus back to your breath.*
2. ***Body Scan:*** *Start at the top of your head and slowly scan through your body. Notice if you feel any tension or discomfort. With each breath, imagine that stress melting away, leaving you relaxed.*
3. ***Thought Observance:*** *Picture your thoughts like clouds in a vast sky. Acknowledge each thought without judgment and let it pass by. If you get caught up in thoughts, gently return your attention to the present moment.*

These exercises can help you become more mindful and present daily, promoting inner peace and self-awareness.

Section 1: Breaking Free from Mental Blocks:

Mental blocks are like invisible walls in our minds that stop us from doing our best. They make us doubt ourselves, fear failing, and think negatively, which keeps us from reaching our potential. But we can break free from these mental blocks, and it's super important for our personal growth:

Step 1: Be Aware of Your Thoughts

- First, notice your thoughts and beliefs that are holding you back.
- These thoughts might come from things that happened in the past or what people around you say.
- When you see these thoughts, you can start to change them.

Step 2: Believe You Can Get Better

- Know that you can get more intelligent and better at things.
- Think of challenges as chances to learn and grow, something you can only do.

Step 3: Change Negative Thoughts

- Stop negative thoughts and replace them with positive ones.
- For example, if you think, "I'm not good enough," tell yourself, "I can learn and do better."

Step 4: Picture Success

- Imagine yourself doing well and beating obstacles.
- This makes you feel more confident and ready to succeed.

Step 5: Get Support

- Be around people who make you feel good and support you.
- Share your dreams and challenges with them, or even do it yourself. Both ways are okay.
- This book can be like a friend to help you on this journey.

Step 6: Be Kind to Yourself

- Remember that setbacks are part of learning.
- Be nice to yourself when things are tough, just like you would be to a friend.

Step 7: Take Risks

- Sometimes, you need to do things that feel uncertain or new.
- Don't be scared of change; it's a way to grow.

Breaking free from mental blocks is a significant journey of finding yourself and growing. You can get past these barriers and unlock your true potential with these steps. You'll see many great things you can do when you believe in yourself and keep growing.

Section 2 Embracing Inner Peace:

In mindfulness, we find peace by paying attention to the present. It helps us connect with ourselves and the world around us. Stress and worries don't bother us much, and we feel calm.

Sometimes, our minds are messy with fears and worries that keep us feeling inadequate. But finding inner peace is like cleaning up this mental mess.

Step 1: Self-Acceptance

- Accept that your past mistakes or what you think are your faults don't define you.
- Be kind to yourself, even when you have doubts and fears.

Step 2: Mindfulness

- Focus on your thoughts and feelings without getting too caught up in them.
- This helps clear away negative thoughts and makes space for peace.

Step 3: Forgiveness

- Forgive yourself and others for any wrongs.
- Let go of anger and hurt to feel free and peaceful.

Step 4: Gratitude

- Be thankful for the good things, even in tough times.
- This makes you feel happier and more content.

Step 5: Self-Compassion

- Treat yourself with kindness.
- When you stop criticizing yourself, you'll feel more at ease.

Embracing inner peace is a deep journey of finding yourself and healing. You can let go of negative feelings and discover your inner peace by practicing self-acceptance, mindfulness, forgiveness, and gratitude. This path helps you become your true self and feel calm and happy.

Personal notes: In life, the most critical time is right now. Open your heart and mind to it because life happens in this moment. Don't carry past burdens or future worries; fully enjoy what's happening now. This moment is a gift. It lets us enjoy life, understand the world, and appreciate ourselves. Treat the present like a precious treasure because you'll find peace, purpose, and a strong connection with your true self in its beauty.

Activity 7.2: Mindful Observation.

This simple activity will help you truly embrace the present moment's essence. Find a quiet and comfortable space where you can sit undisturbed for a few minutes. Take a few deep breaths to center yourself and bring awareness to the present moment.

Choose an object nearby, such as a flower, a piece of fruit, or any small item that catches your eye. Hold the object in your hands or place it in front of you on a table.

Now, observe the object mindfully, using all your senses. Notice its shape, color, texture, and any unique details. Please take a moment to feel its weight in your hands or sense its presence before you. Inhale its fragrance or take a moment to appreciate its taste if it's edible.

Allow yourself to be fully present with the object, immersing yourself in this moment of mindful observation. If your mind wanders or thoughts arise, gently guide your focus back to the thing. Spend a few minutes fully engaged with the object, embracing the present moment with curiosity and openness. When you feel ready, slowly release your focus from the object, taking a few deep breaths to ground yourself in the present moment.

This activity helps you experience the depth and richness of the present moment through mindful observation. It encourages you to immerse yourself fully in the now, free from distractions and preoccupations. By regularly practicing conscious observation, you will develop a deeper appreciation for the beauty and wonder surrounding you, and you'll find it easier to embrace the present moment in all aspects of your life.

CHAPTER 8 SUMMARY: SETTING BOUNDARIES AND PRIORITIZING SELF CARE.

In our busy lives, work, family, and social commitments pull us in many directions. But it's vital to set boundaries and prioritize taking care of yourself. This isn't selfish; it's about looking after your mental, emotional, and physical health.

Setting boundaries means clearly but assertively communicating your limits and needs without feeling guilty. Edges give you personal space and protect your time and energy. They allow you to say 'no' when needed to prevent burnout.

Boundaries also create room for self-care, which is about looking after your well-being. It includes daily rituals like meditation, journaling, and more significant activities like spending time in nature or doing things you love. Self-care is about being kind to yourself and recognizing your worth.

Remember, you don't have to do everything society expects. True well-being comes from balance and harmony. To set boundaries and prioritize self-care, listen to your inner voice, not external pressures. Trust yourself to navigate life wisely.

By setting boundaries and focusing on self-care, you empower yourself and inspire others to do the same. You become a role model for self-love and respect, positively impacting your relationships and community.

This journey of setting boundaries and prioritizing self-care transforms you into a stronger, more resilient, and fulfilled person. It's an act of love and respect towards yourself, recognizing that your well-being matters greatly.

Section 1: Fostering Courage: The Art of Assertive Boundary Communication.

Communication is essential for human connections, and setting boundaries is crucial for healthy relationships. Yet, expressing your needs and limits can be intimidating due to fear, guilt, or a desire to please others. Developing the courage to communicate boundaries assertively is an act of self-discovery and self-advocacy.

To foster this courage, understand that setting boundaries is not selfish but necessary for self-preservation. Boundaries protect your emotional and physical well-being.

Explore the roots of your fear and self-doubt when setting boundaries. Recognize that past experiences or conditioned beliefs may be holding you back. Confront these barriers with compassion and understanding.

Practice self-compassion. Treat yourself kindly to free yourself from guilt and self-criticism. Self-compassion empowers you to speak your truth with love and acceptance.

Learn assertiveness as a skill. Find the balance between firm boundaries and respect for others. Express your needs directly using 'I' statements to foster mutual understanding.

Visualize positive outcomes in boundary communication to build confidence and reduce anxiety. It's like rehearsing for a crucial performance.

Surround yourself with supportive individuals who encourage and validate you. A loving network of friends and loved ones reinforces your worth and the importance of self-advocacy.

As you foster courage in boundary communication, you'll realize it enhances your well-being and nurtures healthier relationships. It's an act of respect for yourself and others, building trust, understanding, and genuine connections.

Building this courage is a challenging but rewarding part of self-discovery and self-empowerment. By recognizing self-care's significance, exploring your fears, embracing self-compassion, developing assertiveness, visualizing positive outcomes, and cultivating a supportive network, you open the door to authentic communication and empowered relationships. Each assertive boundary you set reclaims your power and leads to a life where your needs are honored and your voice is heard with strength and grace. Embrace this journey, for it's a path to authentic self-expression and deeper connections with others.

Section 2: Nurturing the Soul: The Art of Self-Care and Prioritizing Ourselves.

In our busy lives, we often need to remember to take care of ourselves because we're pulled in many directions by responsibilities. Choosing self-care and putting ourselves first is an essential act of self-love and empowerment. It rejuvenates us and equips us with the tools to handle life's challenges.

Self-awareness is the first step in self-care. It means understanding our needs, emotions, and desires without judgment. This helps us recognize when to pause and take care of ourselves.

Creating a personalized self-care routine is a powerful tool. It involves setting aside time for activities that bring us joy and peace, like meditation or journaling.

Setting boundaries is another crucial aspect. Saying 'no' when necessary protects our time and energy, allowing us to focus on self-care without guilt.

Mindfulness, staying in the present moment, is vital for self-care. It helps us find tranquility and recharge, even in life's chaos. Practicing gratitude is transformative. It shifts our focus from what we lack to what we have, fostering contentment and fulfillment. Seeking support and guidance through therapy, coaching, or mentorship can be beneficial on our self-care journey.

Self-care and prioritizing ourselves are essential for a fulfilling life. By cultivating self-awareness, creating a self-care routine, setting boundaries, practicing mindfulness, embracing gratitude, and seeking support, we equip ourselves with the tools to nurture our well-being and spread positivity. Self-care is an act of self-compassion that reminds us we are worthy of love and care. Prioritize yourself, for you hold a treasure within your soul.

Activity 8.1 Cutting the ties.

Warning: This activity might be challenging, so approach it with care and courage. It's crucial for your well-being.

This activity is about setting boundaries and prioritizing self-care by letting go of people who disrespect your boundaries or hinder your growth.

1. **Reflect:** *Think about the people in your life. Identify those who don't respect your boundaries or hold you back from growing. Write down their names and why their presence is harmful to your well-being.*
2. **Acknowledge:** *Be honest about these relationships' impact on your emotional state. Recognize that choosing self-care means prioritizing your well-being over toxic relationships.*
3. **Prepare:** *Understand that cutting ties, though challenging, is a step toward a healthier life. Mentally brace yourself for this emotional process. Remember, this action makes room for positive influences to enter your life.*
4. **Communicate (if possible):** *Have an honest conversation with these individuals. Clearly express your boundaries and your need for space. If direct communication is too hard, gradually reduce your interactions with them.*
5. **Limit Contact:** *Protect your well-being by limiting the time spent with these individuals. Create a healthy distance to nurture your mental and emotional health.*
6. **Seek Support:** *Surround yourself with supportive friends or even just one person who respects your boundaries. Look for role models who inspire you to be your best self.*
7. **Be Kind to Yourself:** *Understand that letting go is challenging. Be gentle with yourself during this process. Remember, you deserve to be surrounded by people who cherish and respect you.*

8. **Embrace Change:** *As you remove toxic influences, make space for new, positive relationships. Embrace this journey of self-discovery, allowing yourself to thrive in an environment that nurtures your well-being.*

Setting boundaries and choosing self-care might involve tough choices but are vital for growth. By letting go of negativity and welcoming positive influences, you're laying the foundation for a life filled with peace, personal development, and the freedom to be your authentic self.

CHAPTER 9 SUMMARIZE CONCLUSION.

As we finish the first volume of "Coffee with My Demons," we're on the brink of an incredible journey toward self-discovery and healing. This initial step has laid the foundation for a transformative process that will lead us to the third volume, where we'll break free from our past and embrace a brighter future.

Throughout this journey, we've explored the various aspects of our inner world - our joys, dreams, mental blocks, and past traumas. Together, we've learned to embrace vulnerability, using it as a powerful tool to face our inner demons with courage and compassion, connecting deeply with our authentic selves.

But remember, this journey is ongoing. The second volume awaits us, where we'll dive deeper into understanding our demons, practicing forgiveness, and nurturing a growth mindset. We'll clean up our mental house through these chapters, making room for resilience and self-empowerment.

Know that I, the writer, am here with you as your unwavering guide and supporter. This journey has its challenges, but it's within these challenges that you'll discover your inner strength and resilience. Every step, every act of self-compassion, and every boundary you set brings you closer to reclaiming your power and unlocking your true potential.

Dear reader, have hope and faith in the journey ahead. The second volume will explore past traumas, older demons in our inner house, self-compassion, and the path to freeing ourselves from our nightmares. Together, we will emerge as masters of our inner home, unburdened by the weight of the past and ready to embrace a life filled with love, joy, and authentic happiness.

Remember, you're not alone on this path. Seek support when needed, surround yourself with those who uplift and inspire you, and hold onto the hope that your life will improve.

Embrace the present, embrace yourself, and know that brighter days are ahead. This journey showcases your courage and resilience, and I'm confident you'll emerge victorious. May the wisdom and insights from this first volume guide you as you continue your transformative journey toward self-mastery and liberation.

Remember, I'm here for you every step of the way. Together, we will triumph, and your inner demons will yield to the brilliance of your authentic self.

BONUS MATERIAL:

Section 1: The importance of nutrition in mental well-being.

The food we eat doesn't just affect our bodies; it also significantly impacts our mental well-being. Eating right can improve our mood, thinking abilities, and overall mental health. On the other hand, a bad diet can make problems like stress, anxiety, and depression worse. Knowing how food and mental health are connected helps us produce intelligent choices for our emotional well-being.

One significant change is to eat whole, nutrient-rich foods. Fill your plate with colorful fruits and veggies packed with vitamins, minerals, and antioxidants. These nutrients are like brain fuel; they keep your brain healthy, reduce inflammation, and help you feel happier. Also, go for whole grains, beans, and lean proteins because they give you steady energy and help make essential brain chemicals.

Cutting back on processed and sugary foods is another big step. These foods can make your mood swing and leave you tired. If you want something sweet, try healthier options like honey or maple syrup, or have some fresh fruits.

Adding omega-3 fatty acids to your diet can also significantly help your mental health. These healthy fats are like brain boosters; they support your brain and make you feel better when dealing with depression or anxiety. You can find omega-3s in fatty fish, chia seeds, flaxseeds, and walnuts.

Lastly, remember to drink enough water. Not drinking enough can make you feel cranky and tired, messing with your mood and thinking. So, stay hydrated to keep your body and mind working their best.

These changes in your eating can significantly affect how you feel mentally. Feeding your body and mind with healthy foods sets the stage for emotional balance, resilience, and greater well-being. And don't forget, even small changes in your diet can improve your mental health, helping you on your journey of "Coffee with My Demons."

Section 2: Sleep

Sleep dramatically impacts how we feel mentally, but it's often overlooked. Good, restful sleep is crucial for our emotions and thinking. While we sleep, our brains do essential things like organizing memories and managing our emotions. But if we don't get enough sleep regularly, it can lead to mood problems, anxiety, and trouble thinking clearly.

Try changing your sleep routine to sleep better and feel mentally more substantial. First, set a regular sleep schedule by going to bed and waking up at the exact times every day, even on weekends. This helps your body get used to a natural sleep pattern. Create a bedtime routine that lets you relax, like reading a book or taking a warm bath. Avoid screens and bright lights at least an hour before bed because they can mess up your sleep hormone, called melatonin.

Make your bedroom comfy, calm, and dark. Get a good mattress and pillows that suit you. If noise bothers you, try using white noise machines or earplugs to block out sounds that might keep you awake.

Sometimes, natural supplements can help improve your sleep and mental well-being. Melatonin is popular; it can help you sleep better, especially if your sleep pattern is irregular or you're dealing with jet lag. Another option is magnesium, which can calm your nervous system and help you relax before bed. But always check with a healthcare pro before trying any supplements to ensure they're safe and suitable for you.

You greatly support your mental well-being when you prioritize sleep and change your sleep habits. Good sleep lets your brain deal with emotions, reduces stress, and prepares you to face challenges and grow. Remember, like other self-care activities, sleep is a powerful tool on your journey to inner peace and self-liberation.

Section 3: Nutraceutical Support

Nutraceuticals, natural supplements, have gained attention for their potential to support mental well-being. Some, like omega-3 fatty acids, Ashwagandha, curcumin, GABA, L-tyrosine, and 5-HTP, have shown promise in reducing stress anxiety and improving cognitive function. Multivitamins can also be beneficial. However, it's essential to consult with a healthcare professional before adding any supplements to your routine. These supplements should complement a holistic approach to mental health, including a balanced diet, exercise, sleep, and professional mental health support when needed. Combining these strategies can enhance your mental well-being on your journey to inner peace and self-discovery.

COFFEE WITH MY DEMONS: PART 2 THE PAST.

Dr. Alec M. Laracuente

Coffee With My Demons Series Vol 2 of 3.

INTRODUCTION: A PAINFULLY BEAUTIFUL HEALING.

Welcome to the next chapter of your journey towards self-discovery and transformation. "Coffee with My Demons Part Two: The Past" will take you on a profound exploration of your past, where you'll encounter shadows and memories that have shaped you. This path may be challenging, but it is also an opportunity for growth and healing.

Within the pages of this volume lies the key to unearthing the secrets that have held you captive for far too long. Together, we'll delve deep into the roots of limiting beliefs, confront past traumas, and address nonadaptive behaviors. This journey may be uncomfortable and evoke emotions you've long kept hidden, but it's a necessary step toward freedom. Remember that you're not alone. Every word, every revelation, and every piece of your story is part of a collective journey toward growth and healing. Each page holds the promise of empowerment, and each activity is a step closer to unshackling yourself from the burdens of the past.

Read on with an open heart, a spirit of hope, and the understanding that this book is a pivotal moment in your transformation. With each uncomfortable conversation, each painful memory, and each step forward, you'll rewrite the narrative of your life. You'll emerge from the shadows, reclaiming the pieces of yourself that were lost and pave the way for a future illuminated by resilience and authenticity.

CHAPTER 1: UNEARTHING THE SHADOWS.

Welcome to Chapter 1, where we embark on self-discovery and introspection. As we enter the realm of our mental house, we are ready to confront the hidden chambers where our deepest fears and limiting beliefs reside. We approach this task with a newfound resolve to shed light on even the darkest corners and to reclaim control over our narrative.

Our mental house is a complex and vast space, holding the memories, dreams, and fears that have shaped us. Each room is a fragment of our journey, revealing the experiences that have influenced our decisions and relationships. Through reflective practices and guided exercises, we begin unearthing the suppressed memories and experiences that have shaped our mental landscape.

As we delve deeper into our mental house, we learn to identify and confront our inner "demons," each carrying a unique story and leaving its mark on our lives. We explore the origins of our fears, anxieties, and self-imposed limitations with compassion, unlocking the levels buried beneath the surface.

Through this process of illumination, we set the stage for profound healing and growth. With every step we take, we inch closer to reclaiming our true selves, unburdened by the shadows of yesterday. Embracing our inner demons, we pave the way for the light of transformation to enter and for a future defined by authenticity, resilience, and liberation.

Welcome to Chapter 1, where we stand at the threshold of profound inner exploration, ready to confront the past with an open heart, eager to embrace the transformation that awaits.

Section 1: Unveiling the Big Five.

Acknowledging the "demons" that hold us back is crucial for personal growth. These internal forces, which I call: "The Big Five," shaped by past traumas, can shape our perspectives and limit our potential. "Regret" can lead to self-doubt, "Abandonment" can make us question our self-worth, "Failure" can distort our view of success, "Insecurity" can leave us vulnerable to criticism, and "Trauma" can affect our overall well-being. However, we can liberate ourselves and achieve great things by confronting these demons head-on and working towards healing and growth. It's a challenging journey but one that offers immense rewards.

Activity 1.0: Mapping Your Big Five.

1. **Create Your Inner Demon Map:** *Start by using the space provided and drawing a simple house map. Divide the house into five rooms, each representing a different aspect of your mental landscape. Label these rooms as "Regret," "Abandonment," "Failure," "Insecurity," and "Trauma."*
2. **Reflect on Each Room:** *Take a moment to reflect on each room and the associated one of the five. Think about instances in your life when you've felt the impact of these demons. Have some specific events or experiences triggered these feelings? Write a brief description or*

keyword next to each room to represent your understanding of the demon's presence.

3. **Rank Their Influence:** *On a scale of 1 to 10, rate the level of influence each demon has over your daily life. Consider how often they surface, how much they affect your thoughts and behaviors, and the degree of distress they cause. This step will help you clarify which demons may be the most prevalent and impactful for you.*

4. **Identify Common Triggers:** *Explore what situations, memories, or circumstances trigger these demons' appearance. Are specific events or patterns consistently leading to feelings of regret, abandonment, failure, insecurity, or trauma? Write down a few critical triggers for each demon.*

5. **Consider Their Interactions:** *Reflect on how these inner "demons" interact. Do you notice any patterns or relationships between them? For example, does a sense of failure often trigger feelings of insecurity? By understanding these interactions, you can better comprehend the interconnected nature of your inner demons.*

6. **Set a Compassionate Intention:** *As you complete this activity, set an intention to approach confronting these "demons" with self-compassion and a commitment to healing. Acknowledge that this is a courageous step towards self-awareness and growth.*

By completing this activity, you'll have a clearer understanding of the "Big Five" that may be holding you back. This knowledge is a crucial foundation for the next steps in your journey toward self-transformation as you delve deeper into addressing these powerful adversaries. Remember, you're not alone in this process; every step you take brings you closer to reclaiming your mental well-being. DO NOT spend additional time in this big five now, as we will eventually take on each of them. Before I explain, the weapons will be used against the big five and any other remanent demons in your inner house.

Activity 1.0: Unveiling Your Big Five.

_____
_____
_____
_____
_____
_____
_____
_____
_____
_____
_____
_____
_____
_____
_____
_____
_____
_____
_____
_____
_____
_____
_____
_____
_____
_____
_____

CHAPTER 2: UNLEASHING THE POWER OF SOUL RETRIEVING.

As we aim to deal with the things inside us that trouble us, let's use more friendly terms like "internal conflicts" or "areas of opportunities" instead of "demons" so often. We're going to explore something ancient and powerful called soul retrieving. This technique might help us find parts of ourselves that we've lost. It can help us face our past, heal old wounds, and break free from our inner struggles. Through soul retrieving, we're on a more profound journey to discover ourselves, to bring back parts we've forgotten, and to become whole again.

Understanding Soul Retrieving: At its core, soul retrieving is a personal journey into the realms of our psyche, guided by our inner wisdom. While it can be incredibly beneficial to seek the guidance of skilled practitioners, it's also a practice that you can explore on your own with the guidance of this and other books; I dearly love the work of Alberto Villoldo, Ph.D. in his book *Mending the past & healing the future with Soul Retrieval*. Begin by creating a sacred space where you feel safe and connected. This could be a quiet room, a tranquil natural spot, or even a cozy corner where you can meditate and reflect.

The Journey: in all the healing tools provided in this book, you can start by focusing on a specific moment that felt particularly challenging or traumatic. This could be an event from your childhood, an experience that left a deep emotional scar, or a recurring pattern of behavior that you're struggling to understand. As you hold this memory, gently ask yourself, "What part of my soul did I lose during that time?" Trust your intuition; you may feel a sense of disconnect, a missing piece, or a suppressed emotion.

Integration: Once you identify this soul fragment, imagine reaching it with love, compassion, and understanding. Invite this fragment to return to you, knowing it holds valuable lessons and strengths essential to your wholeness. This might take time and patience, but be persistent. Allow the fragment to merge with you, feeling a sense of completeness and reconnection. It's like welcoming back an old friend, acknowledging its significance in shaping who you are today.

Facing the "internal conflicts": Soul retrieving is a powerful tool for our battle against the "internal conflicts." As we recover these lost aspects of ourselves, we understand the origins of our fears, insecurities, and limiting beliefs. We shed light on the rooms in our mental house where these demons have taken refuge. By acknowledging these hidden aspects, we prepare ourselves to confront them with compassion, strength, and resilience.

Dispatching the Demons: With these lost soul fragments re-integration, we become better equipped to face our inner "inner demons" head-on. Each retrieved piece of our soul contributes to dismantling the power these "internal conflicts" once had. As you serve the table for having coffee with your "demons," engage with them in a dialogue, a process of understanding their origin, their role, and the lessons they have brought you. With the new-found wholeness, wisdom, and resilience cultivated through this process, you compassionately dispatch them, releasing their grip on your life.

In the chapters, we will explore the practice of soul retrieving as others, providing guided exercises and practical techniques to harness its transformative power. As you embrace the depths of your past, reclaiming the fragments of your soul, you pave the way for the ultimate liberation from your inner "demons." The journey will be intense, but the rewards are immeasurable—a path toward healing, growth, and the triumphant emergence of your authentic self.

CHAPTER 3: EMBRACING AND CONFRONTING THE DANCE OF REGRET.

The mind is an easy-to-get-lost place, and many things happen without going unnoticed. One of these things is the impact of having regrets. Regret is a deep-rooted debilitation internal struggle that has reached every part of our mind, especially if left unchecked.

Section 1: The Birth of Regret.

Few emotions hold as much sway as regret. It is a multifaceted phenomenon that impacts our aspirations and the fabric of time. Regret is not a singular event; it is a process, a living entity that emerges from the crossroads of possibility and can shape our perceptions, behaviors, and even our lives.

The genesis of regret lies in the realm of possibility—a garden of dreams and desires. Each decision we make, every path we choose, bears within it the weight of potential alternative outcomes. These unexplored avenues whisper to us, tempting us with the allure of what could have been. In the fertile soil of possibility, regret's seeds take root, growing as we contemplate the road not taken, the unsaid words, and the choices that diverged from our current reality.

Our life journey is a mosaic of choices, and regret finds its foothold among them. It often emerges from pivotal moments where we stood at the crossroads, hesitating, deliberating, and ultimately making a decision that set us on a particular course. Regret doesn't stem solely from bad choices; it can also arise from the profound weight of unchosen paths, those tantalizing branches that beckon with the promise of alternate destinies. It's the job not pursued, the relationship not nurtured, the adventure not embarked upon—the layers of life we didn't explore.

The specter of "what-ifs" is where regret takes hold, haunting us with echoes of different outcomes. These "what-ifs" cast their enchanting spell, fueling our imagination with scenarios where we imagine a brighter, more satisfying existence if only we had chosen differently. The roads not taken, the unspoken feelings, the dreams left unfulfilled—they linger in the corridors of our minds, carried by the whispers of regret.

Consider the individual who once had the opportunity to chase a dream to pursue a passion, but the practicalities of life led them to choose a more conventional path. As time marches, regret may emerge as they witness others achieving what they once aspired to. Regret accompanies them as they see others thrive in the arena they once envisioned for themselves. It's a quiet but persistent reminder of the roads untaken, a shadow of what could have been.

Understanding the birth of Regret is to peer into the intricate dance of choice, possibility, and the eternal pull of the "what-if." It's a profoundly human experience, an emotion that highlights our capacity for reflection, aspiration, and the gnawing feeling that we are the architects of our own life stories. Yet, within this understanding, there lies a profound opportunity. Regret, while often seen as a precursor of sorrow, can be a catalyst for growth, a teacher that guides us toward a more mindful, purposeful existence.

As we traverse the corridors of our inner house, exploring the chambers of regret, we embark on a journey of self-discovery. Through introspection, self-compassion, and the transformative power of learning from our choices, we can untangle the threads of regret, weaving them into the fabric of wisdom. The past does not bind us; instead, it empowers us. Regret, in all its complexity, can become a stepping stone toward a life imbued with resilience, compassion, and the audacity to carve our path.

In the depths of our regret, we uncover the resilience of the human spirit. The spark pushes us to reflect, evolve, and embrace the lessons we gather. Regret becomes not a prison of the past but a bridge to our future selves. Through understanding, acceptance, and the gentle guidance of self-compassion, we learn that regrets need not define us but can serve as catalysts for transformation. We reclaim our agency, navigating the winding roads of life with newfound purpose, embracing the beautiful, imperfect mosaic of our choices, and charting a course toward a future infused with intention, growth, and the unwavering hope that every step taken, regretted or celebrated, propels us forward on this remarkable journey of existence.

Section 2: The Impact on Our Inner House, Unmasking Trades, and Behaviors.

Regret is like a shadow from the past that becomes part of our lives. It marks how we think, act, and deal with others. It's like an "area of opportunity" inside us, quietly affecting how we see things and our choices. When we look at people dealing with regret, we see how it affects them differently.

One of the most striking traits of those trapped by the clutches of regret is a constant dance with the "what-ifs." They ruminate over past choices, replaying the pivotal moments when a different decision could have led to an alternative reality. These individuals become collectors of missed opportunities, accumulating a mental inventory of the roads not taken, the unsaid words, and the dreams that slipped through their fingers. The "what-ifs" hang like a shadow, a persistent reminder of the branches of life that could have led to brighter horizons.

Another hallmark behavior of those touched by Regret is a delicate balancing act between nostalgia and longing. They often find themselves reminiscing, seeking solace in the moments when life felt simpler, choices less daunting. This longing for a bygone era is interwoven with a yearning for second chances and a genuine desire to turn back the clock and rewrite the script of their lives. It's as if they are caught between two worlds, the present and the past, unable to fully embrace the present moment due to the ever-present specter of "if only."

In the presence of regret, decision-making becomes a delicate dance, often plagued by hesitation and self-doubt. Those harboring regrets may resist making choices, fearing that history might repeat itself. Every decision carries the weight of past regrets, a reminder of the times when different paths led to disappointment. This hesitancy, born from the desire to avoid future regrets, can sometimes paralyze them, preventing them from fully embracing new opportunities or taking bold leaps.

Furthermore, people living with regrets often struggle with self-compassion. They may be excessively critical of themselves, holding their past actions to an impossibly high standard. This self-judgment becomes a constant companion, whispering reminders of missed chances and mistakes made. This critical inner voice can erode self-esteem, fostering feelings of inadequacy and unworthiness.

However, it's crucial to recognize that these traits and behaviors are not insurmountable barriers but rather signposts on the road to growth and healing. The presence of regret, though challenging, reveals the capacity for reflection, the yearning for change, and the innate desire to shape a life of meaning. By embracing self-compassion, nurturing a growth mindset, and engaging in the transformative journey of self-discovery, individuals can navigate the intricate threads of regret, weaving them into a tapestry of resilience, wisdom, and hope. Refer to the book 1 for these tools.

The road ahead is one of self-compassion and empowerment. It is a path where the lessons of regret are honored but not allowed to define us. It is a journey that demands courage, a willingness to confront the past, and an unwavering commitment to shaping a future filled with purpose. As we explore the trades and behaviors of those living with regret, let us also celebrate the resilience within, the potential for growth, and the power of embracing our imperfect yet beautiful human journey. In this exploration, we uncover the depths of regret's impact but the remarkable capacity of the human spirit to rise above, transform, and forge a path toward a brighter, more fulfilling existence.

Activity 3.1: Exploring the Trade-offs of Regret.

In this activity, we'll explore the trade-offs associated with regret. By examining the decisions that led to regret and the potential gains from alternative choices, you'll gain valuable insights into the impact of regret on your life.

Instructions:

1. *Identify Regretful Moments: Think about moments when you felt regret. These could be decisions you made, actions you took, or opportunities you missed. Choose a few significant regretful moments that stand out.*

2. *Break Down the Decisions: For each regretful moment, break down the decisions that led to it. What choices did you make that you later regretted? Try to understand the context, motivations, and factors influencing those decisions.*

3. *List the Gains: Now, imagine the alternative choices you could have made in each situation. List the potential gains or positive outcomes that could have resulted from those alternative decisions. Consider both short-term and long-term gains.*

4. *Reflect on the Trade-offs: For each regretful moment, reflect on the trade-offs. What did you gain or lose due to the decision that led to regret? Compare the short-term satisfaction or ease with the potential long-term benefits you might have missed.*

5. *Consider Lessons Learned: Regret can be an influential teacher. What lessons have you learned from these regretful moments? How can you apply these lessons to future decisions? Focus on the wisdom gained from the experience.*

6. *Set Future Intentions: Set intentions for the future based on your reflections. Identify areas where you want to make different choices, considering the potential trade-offs. Aim to make decisions that align with your long-term goals and minimize the likelihood of future regrets.*

7. *Practice Self-Compassion: Throughout this activity, practice self-compassion. Regret is a natural part of life, and everyone experiences it. Be gentle with yourself as you explore these moments and focus on using the insights to grow.*

By engaging in this activity, you're identifying the trade-offs of regret and empowering yourself to make more informed decisions moving forward. The lessons from your regretful moments can guide you toward a future where you make choices aligned with your values, aspirations, and long-term well-being.

- *Consider reviewing and repeating activity 3.1, Self-Compassion, from Volume 1.*

Healing Tool 3.1: Regret Resonance Therapy.

Regret Resonance Therapy is an innovative and holistic approach to addressing and healing the impact of regret, inspired by a combination of advanced psychotherapeutic techniques, neuroplasticity principles, and mindfulness practices.

Methodology:

1. **Regret Identification**: The first step in this therapy is to identify the specific regrets affecting the individual. Which we did in activity 3.1 and may go further as and if we find new regrets in our lives.
2. **Regret Exploration**: Once the key regrets are identified, explore the origins and triggers of each regret. This involves delving into the circumstances, decisions, and emotions surrounding those moments, also in activity 3.1.
3. **Neuroplasticity Techniques**: Regret Resonance Therapy leverages the brain's capacity for neuroplasticity. Many of the practices explained in the first volume are already tools of neuroplasticity. Still, I want to introduce cognitive

restructuring techniques for this volume to shift the perspective on past events.

4. **Question the Beliefs**: Take each regretful thought and ask yourself: "Is this belief based on facts, or do my emotions influence it?" Look for evidence that supports or refutes each belief. Consider alternative perspectives and experiences that provide a more balanced view.

5. **Challenge Distortions**: Many regretful thoughts contain cognitive distortions, such as black-and-white thinking, overgeneralization, or personalization. Identify any distortions within your regretful thoughts and challenge them. Ask yourself if there are shades of gray or if the situation is as catastrophic as it seems.

6. **Replace with Rational Responses**: Create a rational and balanced response for each regretful thought. Focus on what you've learned from the experience, even if it's challenging. Consider the growth, resilience, and wisdom gained as a result. Aim to reframe the thought into a more constructive and less self-critical statement.

7. **Practice Self-Compassion**: Remind yourself that everyone makes mistakes and regrets are a natural part of life. Treat yourself with kindness and compassion, as you would a friend who is struggling. Please acknowledge that you're human and regrets are okay; what matters is how you handle them now.

8. **Letting Go Ritual**: Create a symbolic ritual to let go of each regret. This could involve writing down the regret on a paper, reflecting on the lessons learned, and then physically tearing up or burning the paper. This act can symbolize releasing the burden of regret and making space for growth.

9. **Future Focus**: Channel your energy into actionable steps for the future. Set goals and intentions that align with your values and aspirations. Shift your focus from dwelling on past regrets, creating a positive and fulfilling path ahead.

10. **Consistent Practice**: Engage in this cognitive restructuring exercise whenever regretful thoughts arise. Over time, it will become more natural to reframe these thoughts and redirect your mental energy toward a more constructive mindset.

By consistently applying these cognitive restructuring techniques, you'll gradually diminish the power of regret over your thoughts and emotions. Embrace the opportunity for growth and self-compassion, and remember that each day is a chance to shape a more positive and fulfilling future.

1. **Mindfulness Integration**: Mindfulness practices are incorporated to help the client cultivate a non-judgmental awareness of their regrets. Mindfulness meditation allows individuals to observe their regretful thoughts and feelings without getting overwhelmed, leading to reduced emotional intensity over time.

2. **Emotional Release**: Emotional release techniques can help you process and release pent-up regret-associated emotions. While this self-guided exercise can be effective, it's essential to be mindful of your emotional well-being, and seeking the support of a mental health practitioner is beneficial, especially if regret is overwhelming. Here's a simple emotional release technique to help you navigate regret:

Find a Quiet Space: Choose a quiet, comfortable space where you won't be disturbed. This allows you to focus on the process without distractions.

Close Your Eyes and Focus on Breathing: Close your eyes and take a few deep breaths to center yourself. Feel the rhythm of your breath, and let go of any tension in your body.

Identify the Regret: Gently bring the regretful memory or thought to your awareness. Allow yourself to feel the emotions associated with it. Acknowledge the regret without judgment.

Create an Emotional Container: Imagine creating a container in your mind, a safe space to place the emotions connected to the regret. Visualize this container, whether a box, a cloud, or another symbol representing containment.

Transfer Emotions: Slowly transfer the emotions associated with the regret into the container you've created in your mind. As you do this, acknowledge the feelings but let go of their hold on you. Imagine the emotions flowing from your body into the container.

Close the Container: Imagine closing the container securely once you've transferred the emotions. This act symbolizes that you're releasing these emotions from your immediate awareness.

Breathe and Reflect: Take a few more deep breaths and allow yourself to feel the weight lifted from the regret. Reflect on the experience and offer yourself self-compassion. Remind yourself that it's okay to feel regret, but you're taking steps to release its hold on you.

Future-focused Reprogramming: To break free from regret's hold, we can use a powerful tool called "mental contrasting." This technique helps us understand our past choices and brings clarity. It can lead to healing and growth. Using mental contrasting well can help us let go of regret and change how we see things to move forward without the burden of what might have been.

The initial step in this transformative process involves facing regret head-on. We must acknowledge the specific actions, decisions, or missed opportunities that have fueled our feelings of remorse. By confronting these instances honestly and without judgment, we open the door to self-compassion and the potential for redemption. It's essential to understand the impact of these regrets, recognizing how they have affected our lives and the lessons they hold.

Visualization, a potent technique, can be harnessed to free ourselves from regret. Close your eyes and imagine a scenario where you've made different choices and taken a different path, leading to a more positive outcome. Visualize the sense of relief, the freedom from regret, and the feelings of empowerment that come with this alternative reality. Engage all your senses—see the vivid details, feel the emotional liberation, and create an immersive experience within this optimistic vision.

However, overcoming regret often involves reconciling the past with our present circumstances. This is where mental contrasting truly shines. In this step, we pivot our focus back to our current reality, acknowledging the consequences of our past decisions. It's not about dwelling in guilt or self-blame but about being honest with ourselves and taking responsibility for our actions.

The beauty of mental contrasting emerges from the contrast itself—the juxtaposition of our positive vision with the present reality. This contrast, while challenging, allows us to see the disparity and recognize the growth that has occurred since those regretful moments. It encourages us to learn from the past, to gain insights from our experiences, and to channel that wisdom into positive action.

Implementation intentions are born from this contrast, bridging our vision of a regret-free future and our current reality. These specific if-then statements outline our approach to dealing with situations that may trigger regret. They serve as a proactive strategy, helping us navigate moments of potential remorse with grace, intention, and actionable steps. These intentions become our compass, guiding us through the labyrinth of life.

In this process, mindfulness and self-compassion play pivotal roles. We keep our vision of a life unburdened by regret at the forefront, a beacon of hope illuminating our path forward.

Simultaneously, we stay aware of our present reality, acknowledging the growth we've experienced and the opportunities for positive change that exist in the present moment. When faced with moments of potential regret, we turn to our implementation intentions, taking decisive action grounded in our newfound wisdom.

Persistence and patience are vital as we navigate this journey. We may encounter moments where regret resurfaces, but armed with the tools of mental contrasting and implementation intentions, we face them with resilience. We recognize that healing from regret is not a linear path but a continuous learning and growth process. Through this ongoing dance between our vision of a regret-free future and the complexities of our present reality, we find the strength to release the grip of regret and embrace the present with renewed hope.

In essence, mental contrasting with implementation intentions is a comprehensive approach to overcoming regret. It's about coming to terms with our past while channeling the wisdom gained into positive actions in the present. By harnessing this technique, we embark on a journey of self-forgiveness, empowerment, and personal growth. We reframe our perspective on regret, viewing it as a teacher rather than a tormentor, and use its lessons to craft a life free from the burdens of the past.

With mental contrasting as our guiding compass, we find the courage to release regret's hold on our lives. As we navigate the intricacies of this transformative process, we recognize that it requires dedication, self-compassion, and a belief in our capacity for growth. We harness the immense power of our minds to heal from the regrets that have weighed us down, turning them into stepping stones towards a future where regret no longer dictates our choices. Through mental contrasting, we unlock the potential to embrace each day with clarity, purpose, and the freedom to create a life we're proud of.

1. **Integration and Closure**: The therapy concludes with a phase of integration, where you, the reader, reflect on the healing journey and its impact on your emotional well-being. They are empowered to move forward, armed with newfound resilience and self-compassion.

Regret Resonance Therapy is a powerful tool for addressing and healing regret, allowing individuals to free themselves from past burdens and create a more fulfilling and empowered future. By combining elements of psychotherapy, neuroplasticity, mindfulness, and emotional release, this innovative approach offers a comprehensive and holistic healing experience.

Healing tool 3.2: Embracing Soul Retrieving to Overcome Regret.

Regret can be a heavy burden, but through soul retrieving, we can find the pieces of ourselves lost in the past and reassemble them into a stronger, more resilient version of who we are today. This self-guided exercise aims to gently guide you through soul retrieving to release the grip of regret and reclaim the vital energy that may have been scattered in the wake of past choices.

Step 1: Creating a Safe Space.
Find a quiet and comfortable space where you won't be disturbed. Take a few deep breaths to center yourself, creating a safe and inviting environment for this soul-retrieving journey.

Step 2: Visualization of Lost Aspects.
Close your eyes and imagine a beautiful, serene landscape symbolizing your inner world. Visualize aspects of yourself, energy fragments, or parts of your soul scattered across this landscape. These are the pieces that might have been lost due to regret.

Step 3: Call to the Lost.
In your mind, gently call out to these scattered aspects of yourself, inviting them to return to you. Use affirming and loving language, such as, "I welcome back all the pieces of my soul I've lost to regret. You are safe, loved, and wanted."

Step 4: Reintegration.

As you call out, imagine these lost aspects gradually returning to you, merging into your being. Feel the warmth and sense of wholeness as each piece returns, filling you with newfound vitality and strength.

Step 5: Forgiveness and Release.

Now, turn your focus to the source of your regret. Acknowledge the past choices that have led to this regret and offer yourself forgiveness. Understand that you made the best decisions you could at that time. Visualize yourself, releasing the weight of regret, letting it dissolve into the air, freeing you from its hold.

Step 6: Affirmation.

With your regained wholeness and the release of regret, affirm your intention to move forward with a deeper understanding and newfound wisdom. Create a positive affirmation, such as, "I release regret and embrace the lessons it has brought. I am whole, empowered, and ready to live fully in the present."

Step 7: Gratitude and Grounding.

Express gratitude for this healing experience. Take a few moments to feel the connection with your reassembled self and the sense of relief from the weight of regret. When you're ready, slowly open your eyes, bringing this renewed sense of self into your present moment.

Note: Soul-retrieving exercises can be powerful but might bring up emotions that require processing. If you find it challenging or if emotions become overwhelming, it's okay to seek the support of a qualified professional. This exercise is intended as a self-guided tool, and your pace should always prioritize your emotional well-being.

Section 3: The Unveiling of Lesser Demons: A Closer Look at the Ramifications of Regret.

Regret, that formidable inner adversary, is not solitary in its effects on our lives. It spawns a host of lesser "demons," each with its unique expression, yet all interwoven with the threads of our past. As we delve deeper into the realm of these lesser demons, we unearth a complex tapestry of emotions, behaviors, and limiting beliefs that have taken root in the fertile soil of regret.

One of these lesser "demons" born from the depths of regret is "Self-Doubt." It whispers insidiously in our ears, convincing us that our choices are perpetually flawed, leading us to question our judgment in present and future decisions. It wraps us in a shroud of uncertainty, dampening our confidence and eroding our self-worth. We find ourselves hesitating to pursue opportunities, fearing that the outcome will be another regret to add to the pile.

Another companion of regret is "Paralysis of Action." This "demon" shackles us in the grip of indecision, rendering us immobile in the face of new possibilities. It makes us hesitant to take risks or step out of our comfort zones as we repeatedly replay the scenes of past regret in our minds. It stifles our progress, preventing us from fully embracing life's opportunities and reinforcing the cycle of regret as we remain stagnant.

A more subtle "demon," but equally insidious, is "Relationship Tension." Regret can cause us to harbor unresolved feelings towards others or ourselves. These lingering emotions, unaddressed and festering, can strain our relationships. We may find ourselves harboring resentment, unable to fully engage in the present moment, as our minds remain tethered to the past, replaying the scenarios where regret was born.

"Limiting Beliefs" is yet another byproduct of regret's influence. It plants seeds of doubt about our abilities and worthiness. These beliefs manifest in our perceptions of what we can achieve, stifling our growth and keeping us confined to a narrow scope of possibilities. We may find ourselves saying, "I can't do that" or "I'm not good enough," as these limiting beliefs sabotage our aspirations and keep us from realizing our true potential.

These lesser "demons," each born from the initial spark of regret, weave a complex web that can entangle us in a cycle of self-doubt, inaction, strained relationships, and limiting beliefs. Recognizing their presence is the first step toward dismantling their hold on our lives. As we confront each demon, one by one, we begin to unravel the tangled threads and free ourselves from the shadows cast by regret. It is a challenging journey that promises liberation, empowerment, and the eventual ability to confront the most formidable demon of all—regret itself.

Personal Notes:

We just fought the inner "demons" of Regret, the subtle shadows that whisper of missed opportunities and past missteps. Yet, by embracing regret, we uncover the seeds of transformation. We've delved into the depths, unearthing the lesser "demons" born from regret's touch—self-doubt, inaction, strained relationships, and limiting beliefs. We've learned that these demons, though formidable, are not unconquerable.

But remember this: as we journey through the corridors of our regrets, we are not alone. The path we tread has been illuminated by the wisdom of those who've traveled before us and by the strength of countless souls who've faced their inner "demons." We stand at the precipice of liberation with the tools, the knowledge, and the unwavering resilience to rewrite the narrative of our lives.

With its lessons and scars, the past is our springboard, propelling us into a future where regret no longer holds dominion. We can reshape our beliefs, mend strained connections, and move forward with the unshakable conviction that the best version of ourselves is within reach.

With each page turned, each introspective exercise completed, and each commitment to self-growth made, we inch closer to the person we aspire to be. Remember, dear reader, the journey is not without its challenges, but the seeds of our greatest triumphs lie within those challenges. As we forge ahead, may we find the strength to embrace our imperfections, confront our regrets, and believe in the beautiful possibility of becoming our best selves.

The path of self-discovery, healing, and transformation continues, and as we journey forth, let our hearts be filled with hope, our minds with resilience, and our spirits with the unwavering resolve to triumph over regrets, illuminating a path of joy, fulfillment, and growth.

CHAPTER 4: CONFRONTING THE INNER DEMON OF ABANDONMENT.

In one of the other rooms of your inner house lies a formidable specter, an internal "demon" known as abandonment. This shadowy presence, subtle yet potent, often originates in the earliest chapters of our lives. Those moments of neglect, rejection, or the piercing sensation of being left behind shape the foundation upon which abandonment thrives. It subtly finds its way into our existence, influencing our self-perception, relationships, and choices.

Abandonment has a way of shaping our reality, like the lingering echo of a haunting melody. It thrives on the moments when we perceive ourselves as unnoticed or dismissed, etching a lasting impression on our capacity to trust, connect, and fully embrace life's offerings. The growth of abandonment is insidious, akin to an invasive vine that takes hold when least expected. It capitalizes on our vulnerabilities, amplifying feelings of inadequacy and implanting a gnawing fear of being forsaken. As it gains strength, it casts a pervasive shadow over our ability to forge meaningful connections, wholeheartedly pursue our aspirations, and engage in love without the specter of abandonment lurking nearby.

Once entrenched, this inner "demon" manifests in multifaceted ways. It may drive us to push people away, foster an overreliance on self-sufficiency, or sabotage opportunities for genuine connection.

It whispers insidious doubts in our ears, sowing seeds of self-doubt and convincing us that we are undeserving of love and that opening our hearts is an invitation to inevitable pain. But we are not powerless in the face of this relentless adversary. Confronting abandonment is a brave journey of healing, a process where we reclaim our self-worth with unwavering courage. It begins by acknowledging the pivotal moments that breathed life into this demon, tracing its roots back to the experiences that etched it into the very fabric of our being. By summoning the strength to confront these memories, we take the crucial first step toward dismantling Abandonment's suffocating grip.

In the quest to confront abandonment, we embark on a path of self-compassion and self-love. We remind ourselves that we deserve love, connection, and support. We release the vice-like grip of past scars on our present, wresting back the narrative of our lives from the clutches of abandonment.

Throughout this chapter, purposeful activities are woven into the fabric of our journey, guiding us through comprehending the origins of abandonment, challenging its detrimental influence, and ultimately reclaiming our self-worth. As we engage in these activities, we understand that this is a journey of healing, and within us lies the power to triumph over the grip of abandonment.

Together, we confront the demon of abandonment with unwavering resolve, knowing we are inherently worthy of love, connection, and fulfillment. As we journey through the pages of this chapter, let us reclaim our sense of self-worth, taking those initial steps toward fostering meaningful, trusting relationships that enrich our lives. The path may be challenging, but the rewards are immeasurable, drawing us closer to becoming the very best versions of ourselves.

Section 1: The Genesis of Abandonment: Unraveling the Threads of Emotional Neglect.

Abandonment is a complex, deeply rooted inner "demon" born in the crucible of our earliest experiences. It is woven into the fabric of our being through a delicate interplay of circumstances, emotions, and relationships, leaving a lasting impact on our psyche.

The birth of abandonment is often rooted in the early chapters of our lives, during the tender and formative years of childhood. These primary relationships are the foundation upon which our sense of self, security, and belonging are established. However, within this intricate web of human connection, the seeds of abandonment may be sown.

Abandonment often finds its genesis in emotional neglect, which may take various forms. It may arise from parents or caregivers who are physically present but emotionally distant, preoccupied with their concerns, or unable to provide the emotional attunement children crave. This emotional absence creates a void, a sense of not being seen, heard, or understood—an experience that can be indelibly imprinted on the developing psyche.

Abandonment can also be born from more overt forms of neglect or trauma. The emotional fallout of such experiences reverberates within us, shaping our beliefs about the worthiness of love and our ability to form lasting, meaningful relationships.

Understanding the birth of abandonment is essential for our journey of healing and growth. With this understanding, we can embark on a path of self-compassion, untangling the threads of abandonment and working to rewrite the narrative of our lives.

As we delve into the depths of abandonment's birth, let us approach this exploration with gentleness and a willingness to confront the past. By shining a light on the roots of our inner struggles, we pave the way for healing and nurturing a sense of self-worth not defined by past wounds. As we navigate this complex journey, may we find solace in the knowledge that we can transform our relationship with abandonment, ultimately forging a path toward emotional freedom and a deeper understanding of ourselves.

Section 2: The Mark of Abandonment: Behaviors Woven by Inner Demons.

Abandonment can impact how we behave and see the world. People dealing with abandonment issues might struggle to balance their desire for close relationships with a fear of getting too attached. This struggle can appear in romantic relationships, friendships, or work, where they find it hard to trust and let others in.

Those who carry this inner "demon" may become masters at self-reliance, fiercely guarding their independence as a shield against potential future abandonment. This self-sufficiency may serve as a defense mechanism to protect themselves from the pain of relying on someone, only to face the possibility of being let down once again.

The legacy of abandonment often leaves people with a heightened sensitivity to rejection. This hypersensitivity may lead to overanalyzing interactions, reading between the lines for signs of impending rejection, and even preemptively distancing themselves to avoid the anticipated pain of abandonment.

One of the most challenging behaviors that arise from abandonment is the struggle to trust—trust in oneself, others, and the stability of relationships. People wrestling with abandonment may constantly battle their internal skepticism, often doubting the intentions of others, expecting the worst, and hesitating to fully embrace the beauty of genuine connection.

Recognizing these traits and behaviors as manifestations of a more profound pain grants us the opportunity to confront, embrace, and ultimately transform our relationship with abandonment. With this awareness, we can take on a journey of self-compassion, rewriting the narrative of our lives and forging connections that transcend the shadows of our past. As we walk this path, may we extend the same compassion to ourselves as we would to a dear friend, knowing that healing is possible and pursuing emotional freedom is a courageous endeavor worth embarking upon.

Activity 4.1: Exploring the Shadows of Abandonment.

Objective: This activity aims to help you identify potential abandonment issues within yourself, enabling a deeper understanding of how they might manifest in your thoughts and behaviors. This self-guided exploration is a stepping stone towards healing and growth.

Instructions:

1. **Quiet Reflection:** *Find a peaceful and comfortable space where you won't be disturbed. Take a few deep breaths to center yourself. Close your eyes and focus on your thoughts.*
2. **Trace Your Past:** *Reflect on your early life experiences, particularly those related to relationships, family, friendships, or any significant changes. Allow yourself to journey back to your formative years and recall moments that might have influenced your sense of abandonment. These could include relocations, losses, separations, or instances where you felt left behind or disconnected.*
3. **Emotional Exploration:** *Consider any emotions that arise as you delve into your past. Did you feel sadness, fear, anxiety, anger, or*

confusion during these moments? Take note of the intensity of these emotions and how they might have affected your perception of relationships and trust.

4. **Patterns in Present:** *Now, shift your focus to the present. Observe any recurring patterns or behaviors that might relate to abandonment issues. This could involve a tendency to pull away from relationships when they become too close, an inability to trust others, or heightened sensitivity to perceived rejection fully. Be honest with yourself and avoid judgment.*

5. **Triggers and Responses:** *Think about situations or events that trigger feelings of abandonment. What circumstances tend to amplify these emotions? How do you typically respond when you feel abandoned or rejected? Notice any defensive mechanisms or coping strategies you might employ.*

6. **Personal Reflection:** *Take a few moments to journal your reflections on this activity. Write down specific memories from your past that felt significant, the emotions attached to them, and any present-day patterns or behaviors related to abandonment.*

7. **Compassion and Understanding:** *As you review your reflections, be kind to yourself. Remember that acknowledging and exploring these issues is a courageous step toward growth and healing. Please recognize that these feelings and behaviors are responses to past experiences, and it's within your power to work through them.*

8. **Seek Professional Support (optional):** *If you find that your exploration uncovers deep-seated and challenging abandonment issues that you feel ill-equipped to handle alone, consider seeking the support of a mental health professional. A therapist can provide tailored guidance and tools to help you navigate these complex emotions and work toward healing.*

Remember, this activity is a starting point. Understanding and addressing abandonment issues takes time and patience. Be gentle with yourself and take this opportunity to embark on a journey of self-compassion and growth, knowing that each step brings you closer to healing the wounds of the past.

Healing Tool 4.1: Embrace and Release Abandonment.

Objective: This advanced healing tool combines holistic and mindfulness techniques to address the inner "demon" of abandonment. It aims to help you acknowledge, process, and release the emotional burdens associated with abandonment, fostering healing and creating space for emotional growth.

Instructions:

1. **Prepare a Sacred Space:** Find a quiet and comfortable space where you won't be disturbed. Create a soothing environment with soft lighting, calming scents (such as lavender or chamomile), and perhaps some gentle background music if that helps you relax.

2. **Grounding and Relaxation:** Begin by grounding yourself. Sit or lie down in a comfortable position, closing your eyes. Take a few deep breaths, inhaling deeply through your nose and exhaling slowly through your mouth. Imagine roots extending from your body into the earth, connecting you to its steady and nurturing energy.

3. **Invoking Self-Compassion:** Visualize a warm, golden light surrounding you, representing self-compassion and love. Allow this light to permeate every part of your being, embracing you in a cocoon of acceptance and understanding.

4. **Acknowledging Abandonment:** With a gentle and non-judgmental awareness, invite the memories or emotions related to abandonment. Allow them to surface, observing them as if they were drifting by, without attaching any judgment or labels.

5. **Visualizing the Healing Process:** Imagine holding these emotions in your hands like fragile pieces of glass. As you hold them, acknowledge the pain they carry and the impact they've had on you. Now, visualize a serene lake or river in

front of you. With each breath, release a piece of the emotional burden into the water, watching it dissipate and merge with the current.

6. **Self-Validation:** As you release each piece, repeat a self-affirmation. For example, "I acknowledge the pain of abandonment, but I am not defined by it. I am worthy of love and belonging." Use your own words or choose phrases that resonate with you.

7. **Inner Child Connection:** Visualize your inner child—a younger version of yourself—standing nearby. Approach this child gently, offering comfort, understanding, and reassurance. Let your inner child know they are safe, loved, and deserving of healing.

8. **Forgiveness and Letting Go:** When you feel ready, focus on the person or situation that caused the abandonment. Visualize them before you, and offer them forgiveness, not for their sake but for your healing. Release any resentment or anger, understanding that you deserve freedom from this burden.

9. **Reclaiming Your Space:** Picture the space within you that was once filled with the weight of abandonment now becoming clear and luminous. Fill this space with self-love, self-acceptance, and a sense of wholeness.

10. **Closing the Meditation:** Slowly return your focus to your breath, inhaling and exhaling gently. Feel the present moment, the peace within, and the healing that has begun. When you're ready, open your eyes and take a few moments to reflect on the experience.

Repeat this healing tool as needed, allowing it to guide you on healing and liberation from the inner "demon" of abandonment. Remember, healing is a gradual process, and this tool offers you a profound way to work through and release the emotional wounds that may have held you back.

Healing Tool 4.2: Soul Retrieval, adopt thyself:

Objective: The Soul Retrieval Meditation is a powerful healing tool designed to help individuals reclaim and reintegrate fragmented aspects of their souls that may have been lost due to experiences of abandonment. This self-guided meditation facilitates deep emotional healing, reconnecting the individual with their essence and restoring a sense of wholeness.

Instructions:

1. Preparation: Find a quiet, comfortable space where you won't be disturbed. Sit or lie relaxed, ensuring you feel safe and grounded.
2. Breathing and Centering: Begin by taking a few deep breaths. Inhale deeply through your nose, and exhale slowly through your mouth. As you breathe, imagine a warm, gentle light surrounding you, creating a protective and nurturing space.
3. Guided Visualization: Close your eyes and envision yourself standing in a beautiful, serene landscape, such as a forest, a beach, or a meadow. This landscape represents the realm of your soul, a place where you can retrieve lost aspects of yourself.
4. Meeting Your Soul Guide: Imagine a wise and compassionate spiritual guide appearing in this landscape. This guide represents the wisdom and guidance of your soul. Feel deeply connected with this guide, knowing they are here to support you in this healing journey.
5. Identifying the Fragmented Aspects: With the guidance of your soul guide, begin to explore the landscape. As you do so, you may come across symbolic representations of the fragmented aspects of your soul that were lost due to

abandonment. These may appear as wounded or younger versions of yourself.

6. Reclaiming the Lost Aspects: Approach each fragmented aspect with love and compassion. Imagine embracing and integrating these aspects back into your being. Feel the energy of these lost parts merging with your current self, healing and becoming whole once again.

7. Healing Light Activation: As you integrate each fragmented aspect, imagine a radiant healing light flowing through your entire being, dissolving any residual pain or emotional scars associated with abandonment.

8. Affirmation and Reintegration: Repeat a positive affirmation to yourself, such as "I am whole and complete, deserving of love and belonging." Feel the truth and power of these words resonating within you as you reembrace these lost parts of your soul.

9. Gratitude and Closure: Thank your soul guide for their guidance and support in this healing process. Express gratitude for the reintegration of your fragmented aspects, knowing that you are now on a path of healing and self-discovery.

10. Returning to the Present: Gently open your eyes, carrying the sense of wholeness and reconnection with you. Trust that this soul retrieval meditation has initiated a profound healing process, allowing you to overcome the inner demon of abandonment and move forward with greater self-love and resilience.

Make this Soul Retrieval Meditation a regular practice, allowing it to guide you in reclaiming and nurturing the lost aspects of your soul. As you continue this healing journey, you'll find that the abandonment wounds gradually heal, and you emerge from this process with a renewed sense of empowerment and inner peace.

Healing tool 4.3: Overcoming Abandonment for the More Concrete Mindlike.

Objective: The Abandonment Journal is a concrete and practical healing tool designed for individuals who may find it challenging to engage in meditation but still wish to address and overcome the inner demon of abandonment. This journaling exercise allows for self-reflection, emotional processing, and a deeper understanding of abandonment issues. It may be used to complement the past two meditation healing tools as well.

Instructions:

1. Getting Started: Find a comfortable, quiet space to focus on your thoughts and feelings. Use the writing space provided in this book.
2. Identify Triggering Situations: Identify specific situations, memories, or experiences that trigger feelings of abandonment. These could be events from childhood, relationships, or any situation where you felt left behind or unsupported.
3. Describe Your Feelings: Write how you felt during those triggering situations in detail. Use descriptive language to express your emotions, whether sadness, fear, anger, or any other feeling associated with abandonment.
4. Explore the Impact: Reflect on how these feelings of abandonment have impacted your thoughts, behaviors, and relationships. Note any patterns that you've noticed.
5. Identify Core Beliefs: Explore any limiting beliefs you may hold about yourself, relationships, or the world due to the abandonment experiences. These beliefs can be the root of the inner demon of abandonment.
6. Challenge the Beliefs: Once you've identified these core beliefs, challenge them. Ask yourself whether these beliefs are

based on facts or from past experiences. Consider alternative, more positive beliefs that you'd like to cultivate.

7. Self-Compassion: Practice self-compassion throughout this process. Remind yourself that it's natural to have these feelings, and you're taking a courageous step toward healing by addressing them.

8. Develop a Supportive Narrative: Write a new narrative about your worthiness, self-love, and resilience. Use affirmative statements such as "I deserve love and belonging" or "I am strong and capable."

9. Daily Reflection: Commit to spending a few minutes each day reflecting on your progress, challenges, and any new insights you've gained. This consistent practice helps reinforce your commitment to healing.

10. Celebrate Progress: Acknowledge and celebrate your progress in understanding and addressing your abandonment issues. Each step forward, no matter how small, is a victory on your healing journey.

Using the abandonment tool, you can confront and process feelings of abandonment concretely and structurally. This tool empowers you to identify the root causes of your abandonment issues, challenge negative beliefs, and cultivate a more supportive and compassionate self-narrative. As you continue this healing process, you'll find that the inner demon of abandonment begins to lose its grip, allowing you to embrace a life filled with self-love, resilience, and healthy relationships.

Healing tool 4.3.

Section 3: The Web of Lesser Demons: Navigating Abandonment's Impact.

Abandonment can create many other inner issues that affect us deeply. These issues, like more minor "demons," come from the pain of abandonment. They quietly affect how we see things, how we feel, and what we do. They often work in the background but can significantly impact our lives.

Self-doubt, a close companion of abandonment, weaves a tapestry of uncertainty within us. It emerges from being left behind or unloved, whispering doubts about our worthiness and capabilities. This inner "demon" manifests as a relentless inner critic, questioning our decisions, talents, and fundamental values. It might cause us to downplay our achievements, shy away from new opportunities, or perpetually seek validation from others.

Fear of Rejection thrives on the vulnerability bred by abandonment. It builds emotional walls, encouraging us to keep others at arm's length to shield ourselves from the pain of being rejected once more. This inner "demon" may manifest as social anxiety, making it difficult to forge deep connections, express our authentic selves, or reach out for support. We might find ourselves caught in a cycle of distancing people to evade the perceived inevitability of abandonment.

Emotional Withdrawal, another offspring of abandonment, coerces us to withdraw from our dynamic landscapes. It persuades us to numb our feelings, distance ourselves from emotional experiences, or bury them deep within. This demon can lead to emotional detachment from loved ones, challenging discussing our needs and fears. It may also hinder our ability to express and process emotions healthily, resulting in an unsettling sense of emptiness or detachment.

People-pleasing, a typical response to abandonment, fuels the belief that pleasing others relentlessly will protect us from being left behind. This lesser inner "demon" drives us to prioritize others' needs over our own, often leading to exhaustion, resentment, and a gradual loss of identity. Asserting boundaries, voicing our opinions, or prioritizing our well-being can become arduous tasks as this "demon" guides our actions.

Avoidance, a protective mechanism, emerges as a shield against situations that trigger our abandonment wounds. This "demon" convinces us to sidestep challenging conversations, intimacy, or any scenario with the risk of reigniting feelings of abandonment. It might also deter us from exploring new opportunities, driven by the fear of disappointment or failure. This "demon" perpetuates our comfort zone, stifling growth and limiting our potential.

Relational Patterns imprinted by abandonment can lead to unhealthy dynamics in our relationships. These patterns may involve pushing people away when they get too close or clinging excessively due to a constant need for reassurance. The fear of being abandoned again can profoundly influence our behavior, often sabotaging the connections we yearn for.

Perfectionism emerges as a response to the fear of being unworthy, stemming from the seeds of abandonment. This demon drives us to relentlessly pursue flawlessness in various aspects of our lives, whether our work, appearance, or relationships. We strive for unattainable standards, driven by the hope that we will finally be seen as valuable and lovable if we achieve perfection. However, this constant pursuit often leads to self-imposed stress, anxiety, and a persistent feeling of never being "good enough."

Self-sabotage finds its roots in the lingering doubts sown by abandonment. This inner "demon" subtly influences our actions, causing us to undermine our success or happiness. We may take two steps forward and one step back, sabotaging opportunities, relationships, or achievements when they seem too good to be true. Deep down, we might fear that if we find happiness or success, it will eventually be taken away from us, reinforcing the cycle of abandonment.

Emotional Numbness acts as a protective mechanism against the pain of abandonment. This lesser "demon" encourages us to shut down our emotions, creating a barrier between ourselves and the world around us. We may find it challenging to connect with our feelings, leading to detachment from ourselves and those around us. This emotional numbness shields us from potential hurt but also prevents us from fully experiencing the richness of life's emotional spectrum.

Self-isolation becomes a natural response to the fear of abandonment. This "demon" convinces us that being alone is safer, reducing the risk of being hurt by others. We may withdraw from social interactions, distancing ourselves from friends, family, and potential romantic relationships. The paradox is that while isolation may protect us from the possibility of abandonment, it also perpetuates a sense of loneliness, reinforcing the fear we sought to avoid.

Negative Self-Image takes root from the belief that if we were abandoned, it must have been because something is inherently wrong with us. This "demon" shapes our self-perception, often leading to low self-esteem and self-worth. We may struggle with feelings of inadequacy, constantly comparing ourselves to others and feeling as though we don't measure up. This negative self-image can cascade on various aspects of our lives, from our careers to our relationships.

Escapism becomes a way to cope with the pain of abandonment. This "demon" encourages us to seek refuge in distractions, whether it's excessive work, substance use, or engaging in compulsive behaviors. We may avoid facing our emotions and abandonment wounds by keeping busy or numbing ourselves. However, while providing temporary relief, this escape ultimately prevents us from addressing the core issues that need healing.

Dependency stems from the fear of being left alone, leading us to become overly reliant on others for validation, support, and a sense of identity. This "demon" can result in an unhealthy dependence on relationships, making it difficult to function independently. We may fear asserting our needs or making decisions on our own, fearing that if we do, we'll be abandoned once again.

These lesser "demons," intricate threads woven into our existence, impact how we perceive ourselves, relate to others, and navigate the world. Recognizing their presence is the first step in healing and transformation. By exploring these demons with compassion, self-awareness, and a commitment to growth, we can break free from their hold, allowing us to live authentically, form healthier relationships, and find inner peace.

Personal notes:

As we conclude our exploration of the intricate inner "demon" of abandonment, it's essential to recognize the tremendous courage it takes to confront the shadows that have shaped our lives. We've delved into the depths of the human experience, unearthing the lesser demons that often remain hidden, influencing our thoughts, feelings, and actions. This journey is not for the faint-hearted; it requires resilience, vulnerability, and a willingness to face the past with unwavering determination.

In pursuing self-discovery and healing, we've confronted two metaphorical demons that have held us captive for far too long. We've unveiled the patterns of self-doubt, the fear of rejection, the emotional withdrawal, and the many other manifestations that stem from the profound sense of abandonment. It's an arduous journey to free ourselves from the chains that have restricted our growth and happiness.

But within this journey lies immense hope. The recognition of these "demons" is the first step towards liberation. It's the key that unlocks the door to transformation. It's a reminder that we are not alone in this endeavor, for countless others share in this struggle. We form a community of seekers united by the desire to reclaim our lives, rewrite our stories, and ascend to the heights of our true potential.

Every moment invested in understanding our deep emotions, which we call in this book "demons," is a step towards breaking free from their grasp. Every ounce of self-compassion we extend to ourselves, every boundary we courageously set, and every moment of vulnerability we embrace adds to a life of authenticity, resilience, and emotional freedom. The wounds of the past do not define us; we're shaped by the strength with which we rise above them.

So, let this be an invitation to keep journeying, learning, and growing. The path may be challenging, and the road may be winding, but with each step, we become stronger, wiser, and more aligned with our true selves. In the pursuit of becoming our best selves, we honor the journey, the struggles, and the indomitable spirit within us that refuses to be confined by the shadows of abandonment.

As you turn the pages, remember that you are embarking on a voyage of self-mastery, empowerment, and reclaiming the life you deserve. Each chapter, each exercise, and each moment of reflection brings you closer to the profound healing that awaits. Embrace it, for you have the power to overcome, grow, and create a life defined by your strength, resilience, and limitless potential.

May this wisdom, this insight, and this journey pave the way for a brighter tomorrow. As you move forward, remember that you're not just reading a book but embarking on a transformational odyssey and not alone. Together, we navigate the depths, face the demons, and emerge into the radiant light of self-discovery and wholeness.

CHAPTER 5: EMBRACING THE LESSONS OF FAILURE.

Failure is a standard part of our journey through life. It's something everyone faces. It teaches us things, tests our strength, and sometimes leaves us with hidden wounds. Even though it can be scary, failing at something has important lessons for us to learn. Though daunting, the inner "demon" of Failure carries profound lessons waiting to be uncovered.

When we think of Failure, we often envision it as an adversary, an unwelcome guest threatening our self-esteem and derailing our plans. The shattered dreams, missed opportunities, and unmet expectations shake our confidence and awaken our inner critic. However, beneath the surface, Failure holds the potential for growth, transformation, and the priceless gift of self-discovery.

Failure challenges us to reassess our goals, examine our strategies, and confront the aspects of ourselves that require growth. It's a mirror, reflecting our strengths and weaknesses, inviting us to adapt, learn, and evolve. In the crucible of Failure, we often find the seeds of resilience, courage, and an unyielding determination to rise above the setbacks that once held us captive.

We must recognize that Failure is not a verdict but a chapter in our story. It's a stepping stone, a milestone that marks our progress. Through the trials and tribulations of Failure, we refine our path, recalibrate our ambitions, and forge a deeper understanding of who we are. Each setback has the potential to reveal our true priorities, unveil the core values that drive us, and help us realign our journey with our authentic selves.

The inner "demon" of Failure does not define us; it refines us. It's a compass that guides us toward uncharted territories where innovation and growth thrive. It encourages us to reframe our perception of success to embrace the invaluable lessons that only adversity can provide. It's a gentle reminder that we are human and fallible and that the beauty of our unique journey lies in our imperfections.

This chapter digs into the heart of Failure, exploring its intricacies, impact on our lives, and transformational power. We navigate the emotional landscape of setbacks, dissect the societal expectations that often amplify our fear of Failure, and unearth the hidden gems of wisdom that arise from facing our vulnerabilities.

Through the lens of Failure, we reevaluate our relationship with success, cultivate a resilient mindset, and tap into the wellspring of wisdom that emerges from the scars of our past endeavors. We'll learn to embrace Failure not as a foe but as a formidable ally that propels us forward, strengthens our resolve, and ultimately shapes our life's tapestry into a masterpiece of resilience, growth, and unwavering determination.

As we continue this exploration, let us remember that every chapter, every misstep, and every encounter with Failure is a stepping stone on the path of self-discovery. Together, let us confront this inner "demon" with courage, a willingness to learn, and the understanding that we emerge as the architects of our success by embracing Failure.

Section 1: The Great Master, Failure.

The feeling of Failure doesn't just appear suddenly. It starts quietly, often when we're young. It can come from comparing ourselves to what we see around us. We notice what others achieve and how they're praised for it. At that early age, Failure wasn't a big issue yet. It's more like a slight feeling of not being good enough and uncertainty about what we can do.

As we grow, the expectations placed upon us solidify, whether from family, education, or the ever-pervasive influence of media. The desire to meet these expectations can be overwhelming, and the pressure to succeed intensifies. The inner "demon" of Failure begins to stir as we grapple with the fear of falling short, the dread of disappointing those who hold us dear, and the haunting notion that our worth hinges on accomplishments. This "demon" finds fertile ground in the soil of comparison and societal norms, intertwining its roots with our aspirations, self-esteem, and perception of success.

In our mental house, Failure takes residence and keeps many lesser inner "demons" in his room, including self-doubt and insecurity. It casts a shadow over our dreams, whispering doubts about our abilities, potential, and worthiness. It projects images of past failures on the walls of our minds, replaying them like a never-ending movie, a relentless reminder of our perceived shortcomings. The "demon" of Failure builds barriers, erect walls of hesitation, and manipulates our perception of risk, often preventing us from taking chances and exploring uncharted territory.

Its presence in our mental house can be paralyzing. We hesitate at crucial crossroads, second-guessing our decisions and fearing Failure. Failure can cause us to settle for mediocrity, to avoid pursuing our passions, or to compromise our authentic desires in exchange for the illusion of safety. Its effects ripple through our thoughts, emotions, and behaviors, limiting our potential, stifling our growth, and leaving us trapped in the comfort zone it has cunningly constructed.

Failure, born from the confluence of societal norms, personal expectations, and the fear of falling short, takes residence in the depths of our being. It grows, fed by our insecurities and nurtured by our experiences, until it becomes a powerful force shaping our perception of success and influencing our actions. As we peek into the rooms of our mental house, we must confront this "demon" with compassion, willing to learn from our failures and understanding that Failure is not an end but a stepping stone on the path of growth.

By acknowledging the origins of Failure, understanding its presence in our mental house, and developing a resilient mindset, we can begin the process of liberation. We'll explore how to shift our relationship with Failure, how to reframe it as a teacher, and how to harness its lessons to propel us forward. Through self-compassion, self-reflection, and the courage to confront our fear of Failure, we can transform this "demon" from a tormentor into a catalyst for growth, setting the stage for a life that embraces challenges, learns from setbacks, and ultimately, thrives in the face of adversity.

Section 1: Unresolve Failures, Trades, and Behaviors.

Failure can affect people in many complex ways. It changes how they think, feel, and act. People who carry this burden often feel trapped in a web of self-doubt and fear. They struggle to meet high expectations, which can be challenging for them. Looking closely at their experiences, we see how deeply Failure can affect their lives.

One hallmark trait of those battling Failure is pervasive self-doubt. It whispers constant doubts about their abilities, worth, and potential. This inner voice becomes a harsh critic, questioning their decisions, talents, and even the essence of who they are. It fosters a constant comparison to others, fostering a belief that they must achieve at the same level or risk being deemed inadequate. This self-doubt often keeps them from pursuing their goals wholeheartedly, leading to a life filled with hesitation and second-guessing.

Fear becomes a constant companion for individuals wrestling with Failure. It's not just a fear of Failure itself but a more profound fear of the consequences of falling short. The fear of disappointing loved ones, being judged by society, or facing their inner critique can be paralyzing. This fear drives them to play it safe, avoid taking risks, and settle for mediocrity rather than face the possibility of not meeting the lofty standards they believe are expected of them. This demon's grip on their thoughts and actions keeps them confined within the boundaries of their comfort zone, stifling their growth potential.

The insidious nature of Failure often leads to unhealthy perfectionism as a coping mechanism. Individuals haunted by it strive relentlessly for perfection in all they do, believing that any less than perfection is tantamount to Failure. This pursuit of an unattainable standard can be exhausting, leading to chronic stress, burnout, and even a feeling of emptiness despite their achievements. They may have difficulty celebrating their successes because they constantly raise the bar higher, always chasing an elusive idea of perfection.

Moreover, Failure can foster a tendency to avoid risks and challenges. Rather than facing potential loss head-on, individuals with these traits may choose the safer path, opting for what they perceive as guaranteed success. They may avoid pursuing their true passions, avoid situations where they might fall short, or shy away from opportunities that carry even the slightest hint of risk. This aversion to risk limits their personal growth and prevents them from seizing potential life-changing experiences.

Individuals battling the "demon" of Failure may struggle with vulnerability in their relationships. They may find it challenging to open up about their fears, doubts, and insecurities, fearing judgment or rejection. This can lead to emotional distance from loved ones, as they hide behind a façade of strength, afraid to reveal their inner struggles. The constant fear of failing to meet expectations can also strain relationships, as they may push themselves to the point of neglecting the needs of their loved ones.

It's essential to recognize that these traits and behaviors stem from the insidious presence of the demon of Failure in the mental house of individuals. Acknowledging this demon's role in shaping their experiences is the first step toward healing and liberation.

By fostering self-compassion, challenging unrealistic expectations, embracing vulnerability, and redefining the meaning of Failure, those struggling with the demon of Failure can begin a transformative journey toward self-discovery, growth, and the realization that the absence of Failure does not define their worth, but by their resilience, courage, and the lessons they learn along the way.

Activity 5.1: Exploring the Presence of the Demon of Failure.

In this self-guided activity, we will board a voyage of self-reflection to understand whether the demon of Failure resides within our inner house. This activity will help you identify tendencies, beliefs, or thought patterns associated with this demon. Remember, this is a safe space for self-discovery, and there's no judgment. Let's begin:

Step 1: Find a Quiet Space. *Choose a peaceful environment where you can engage in introspection without distractions. This could be a cozy corner in your home, a serene park, or any place where you feel comfortable.*

Step 2: Self-Reflection: *Take a few deep breaths to center yourself. Reflect on your recent experiences, especially those related to personal goals, achievements, and challenges. Consider the following questions:*

1. *Have there been instances when you hesitated to pursue a dream due to fear of Failure?*
2. *Do you find accepting compliments or celebrating your achievements challenging because you believe they fall short of perfection?*
3. *Have you ever avoided taking risks, even when it could lead to personal growth or a fulfilling experience?*
4. *Do you often feel overwhelmed by self-doubt or an inner critic questioning your abilities and worth?*
5. *Are there specific areas of your life where you constantly set unreasonably high standards, making it challenging to meet your expectations?*

Step 3: Journaling *Use the space provided to make a note to record your thoughts. Answer each of the questions above honestly and in detail. Take your time with this process; take the time to explore your feelings, fears, and experiences.*

Step 4: Analyzing Patterns *Review your answers. Look for patterns or recurring themes in your responses. Are there common threads related to the fear of Failure, self-doubt, perfectionism, or avoidance? Take note of any strong emotions or beliefs that emerged during this exercise.*

Step 5: Self-Compassion and Awareness: *Be kind to yourself as you reflect on your responses. Remember that recognizing the presence of the demon of Failure is a significant step toward healing and growth. It's a* shared experience, and you're not alone. By acknowledging these tendencies, you're already on the path to addressing them.

Step 6: Seek Support (if needed). If you find that the presence of the failure demon impacts your well-being, self-esteem, or quality of life, consider seeking Support from a trusted friend, family member, or mental health professional. They can provide valuable insights, strategies, and encouragement on your journey to overcome this demon.

Step 7: Setting Intentions As you conclude this activity, set an intention to approach situations more self-compassionately, challenge unrealistic expectations, and be open to growth. Remember that the presence of this demon does not define you; it's an aspect that can be acknowledged and transformed through mindful awareness and intentional efforts.

By engaging in this self-guided activity, you've taken a significant step in understanding the presence of the demon of Failure in your inner house. With this awareness, you are better equipped to navigate its impact and embark on healing, self-discovery, and personal growth.

Activity 5.1: Exploring the Presence of the Demon of Failure.

Healing tool 5.1: RISE Model for Overcoming the Inner Demon of Failure.

This self-guided therapy activity will explore the RISE model—an innovative and advanced approach combining Cognitive Behavioral Therapy (CBT), Positive Psychology, and Mindfulness elements. This model is designed to help you overcome the inner demon of Failure by fostering resilience, reframing negative beliefs, and cultivating a growth mindset.

Step 1: Reflection. Take a moment to reflect on a recent experience where you felt like you faced a failure. It could be a professional setback, a personal challenge, or anything that triggered feelings of loss. Write down your thoughts and emotions related to this experience.

Step 2: Identify Negative Beliefs. Analyze the negative beliefs that arose from the Failure. These beliefs might be self-critical, limiting, or filled with self-doubt. Identify the core negative beliefs that you hold about yourself about this Failure. Write them down.

Step 3: Self-Compassion Practice. Practice self-compassion by treating yourself with the same kindness and understanding you would offer a close friend in a similar situation. Write a letter to yourself addressing the negative beliefs you identified in Step 2. Express compassion, understanding, and encouragement to counteract these beliefs.

Step 4: Reframe and Challenge. Using the self-compassion letter as a foundation, reframe the negative beliefs you identified earlier. Challenge them by providing evidence that contradicts these beliefs. Focus on your strengths, past successes, and the lessons you've learned from your failures.

Step 5: Growth Mindset Cultivation: Adopt a growth mindset by recognizing that Failure is essential to learning. Embrace the idea that failures provide valuable insights and opportunities for growth. Write down the lessons you've learned from the recent loss and how it can contribute to your personal development.

Step 6: Gratitude and Positive Focus Shift your focus from the Failure to the positive aspects of your life. Write down three things you're grateful for in the present moment. This practice helps redirect your attention to the present and fosters a positive mindset.

Step 7: Visualization and Future Success Close your eyes and visualize yourself successfully overcoming similar challenges in the future. See yourself confidently navigating obstacles, learning from experiences, and achieving your goals. Engage your senses, emotions, and beliefs in this visualization.

Step 8: Daily Affirmations Create daily affirmations that counteract the negative beliefs you identified earlier. These affirmations should focus on your resilience, growth, and potential. Repeat these affirmations daily to reinforce positive thinking.

Step 9: Continuous Self-Check: Regularly review your progress. Whenever you encounter a setback or face new challenges, apply the RISE model again. Continuously practice self-compassion, reframing negative beliefs, nurturing a growth mindset, and fostering gratitude.

By engaging in this self-therapy activity and consistently applying the RISE model, you're equipping yourself with powerful tools to overcome the inner demon of Failure. This innovative approach integrates the best of various psychotherapy techniques to empower you on your journey toward self-discovery, resilience, and lasting personal growth. Remember, you have the strength within you to rise above the shadows of Failure and embrace the transformative potential it offers.

Healing tool 5.1: RISE Model for Overcoming the Inner Demon of Failure.

Healing tool 5.2: Inner Child Empowerment Journey.

In this healing tool technique, we'll go on an empowering journey to heal the inner child from the clutches of the inner demon of Failure. Combining several therapeutic approaches will create a safe and nurturing environment for the wounded inner child to heal, grow, and reframe its relationship with Failure.

1. **Inner Child Visualization:** Find a quiet and comfortable space where you won't be disturbed. Close your eyes and imagine your younger self—the version of you that experienced moments of Failure. Picture this child with love and compassion, acknowledging their feelings. Visualize wrapping your arms around your younger self, offering comfort and reassurance.
2. **Dialogue with Your Inner Child:** Engage in a heartfelt conversation with your inner child. Ask them about their experiences with Failure, how it made them feel, and what they

needed. Listen attentively to their responses. As an adult, you offer words of understanding, Support, and encouragement, reassuring your inner child that they are valued and loved regardless of past failures.

3. **Reframing Failure:** Help your inner child reframe the concept of Failure. Explain that it's it's natural part of growth and learning. Share examples of successful people who faced failures and setbacks but persevered. Encourage your inner child to see failures as opportunities for growth, not as a reflection of their worth.

4. **Self-Compassion Exercise:** Practice self-compassion by writing a letter to your inner child. In the letter, express your love, understanding, and Support. Acknowledge any pain or disappointment the inner child may have felt due to past failures. Let your inner child know that you're here to guide and protect them and that you believe in their potential.

5. **Empowerment Through Visualization:** Guide your inner child through a visualization of a successful future. Imagine the inner child confidently facing challenges and achieving goals. Encourage the inner child to visualize themselves embracing life, taking risks, and learning from every experience, knowing they are capable of resilience and growth.

6. **Self-Care Rituals for the Inner Child:** Create a list of self-care activities that nurture your inner child. These activities include encouraging hobbies, spending time in nature, engaging in creative play, or simply taking moments to acknowledge and validate your feelings. Incorporate these self-care rituals into your routine to consistently care for your inner child.

7. **Daily Affirmations:** Develop positive affirmations that resonate with your inner child's healing journey. Affirmations like " am worthy of success and growth,"""" embrace challenges with courage and resilience," or " am deserving of love

and support" can be repeated daily to reinforce a positive self-image.

This Inner Child Empowerment Journey is a powerful tool to heal the inner child's wounds from past failures. By nurturing and empowering the inner child with love, understanding, and resilience, you create a foundation for a healthy relationship with loss, enabling you to face challenges with newfound strength and self-compassion.

Personal note:

As we conclude this exploration into the inner" demo" of Failure, I want you to carry with you a message of profound significance. The journey we've embarked upon is not just about overcoming a single obstacle; it's about embracing a transformative mindset that will shape how you perceive challenges, setbacks, and your potential.

Remember, Failure is not a mark of inadequacy but a stepping stone on the growth path. It is the canvas upon which we paint our resilience, where we learn, adapt, and ultimately thrive. Each experience, even the ones that may seem like stumbling blocks, carries the seeds of knowledge and progress.

In this beautiful life, it is not the absence of Failure that defines success but rather the tenacity to rise, learn, and strive forward despite it. Once shackled by the fear of Failure, your inner child realizes that every misstep is a chance to become stronger, wiser, and more compassionate towards yourself.

As you navigate the world, treat yourself with the kindness and understanding you would offer a dear friend. Celebrate your victories, no matter how small, and embrace your setbacks as opportunities for growth. The inner child within you is learning, growing, and evolving with every experience.

Stay open to life's lessons and life that the journey of self-improvement is continuous. Be gentle with yourself, for you are on a courageous path of self-discovery, healing, and empowerment. The inner demon of Failure may have left its mark, but your resilience, determination, and newfound perspective will leave a lasting impression.

Keep moving forward, dear reader, with the understanding that every step, every endeavor, and every challenge is a chance to rise. Any single outcome does not define you; you are determined by your unwavering commitment to becoming the best version of yourself. Embrace your journey with hope, curiosity, and the knowledge that you possess the strength to create a life filled with purpose, growth, and boundless potential.

CHAPTER 6: DEEP DIVING INTO THE COMPLEX LAYERS OF INSECURITY.

Inside our minds, insecurity exists like a hidden shadow. It's not easy to pinpoint, but it significantly affects us. Insecurity isn't confined to one area; it spreads like a mist, touching our thoughts, feelings, and how we see things.

Insecurity resides within every room of our inner house, subtly influencing how we navigate life. It begins its residence in the spaces where doubt and self-criticism first emerge. These could be the chambers where we compare ourselves to others, question our abilities, and harbor fears of not measuring up. The demon extends its reach as time passes, influencing how we interpret our experiences and interactions.

The inner "demon" of insecurity thrives in the chambers where self-worth is questioned. It echoes in the hallways of self-consciousness, where we become acutely aware of how others perceive us. It finds a dwelling place in the corridors of our past mistakes, feeding on regrets and failures. It takes root in the attic of our deepest fears, where the fear of rejection, judgment, or abandonment simmers quietly.

Insecurity doesn't reside in isolation; it interacts with other rooms in our mental mansion. It shares whispers with the "demon" of failure, amplifying each other's messages of inadequacy. It dances with the "demon" of abandonment, fueling fears of being rejected or left behind. And it often exchanges glances with the lesser "demon" of comparison, perpetuating the cycle of measuring ourselves against others.

Insecurity's influence extends beyond individual rooms; it creates connections throughout our mental house. The doubt it sows can permeate every thought and every action. It might alter our perceptions of compliments, causing us to dismiss praise as insincere. It could transform minor setbacks into evidence of our inadequacy. Insecurity distorts the mirrors in our mental house, causing us to see ourselves through a lens of self-doubt.

Insecurity continues to make its presence known; it weaves an intricate web that entangles our self-esteem, relationships, and aspirations. Its tendrils stretch into the corridors of our confidence, eroding our ability to take risks, assert ourselves, or believe in our potential. The more we engage with it, the more it solidifies its hold, dimming our self-assurance and casting a shadow over our sense of identity.

Recognizing this insidious influence is the first step toward reclaiming our mental house from its grasp. By illuminating its existence, we can challenge the distorted beliefs it propagates. Through introspection and self-compassion, we can navigate through the rooms it occupies and dismantle its power. Just as a housekeeper might clear away cobwebs and dust, we can clear the corridors of our minds from the stifling grip of insecurity.

This journey isn't swift or linear; it requires patience, self-reflection, and a willingness to confront our vulnerabilities. Yet, as we unveil the hidden corners of our mental house, dispelling the shadows of insecurity and allowing the light of self-acceptance to flood in. It's an ongoing endeavor that empowers us to reshape our perceptions, build authentic relationships, and forge a deeper connection with our true selves.

Section 1: Birth and Unfolding of Insecurity.

The birth of the inner "demon" of insecurity is a subtle yet profound process, often unfolding in the early stages of our lives and gradually taking residence within the chambers of our inner house. It emerges from a complex interplay of experiences, external influences, and internal perceptions, shaping how we view ourselves and our place in the world.

In its infancy, insecurity often finds its roots in moments of comparison. As children, we observe our surroundings, noticing differences and similarities between ourselves and others. Whether in the classroom, on the playground, or within our own families, these comparisons become the seeds from which insecurity germinates. A sense of not quite measuring up to a perceived standard takes root, fostering the belief that we are somehow lacking or inadequate.

Insecurity also draws strength from external feedback, particularly the opinions and judgments of those around us. Well-intentioned comments from peers, family members, or authority figures can unknowingly contribute to its growth. Words that critique, criticize, or place unreasonable expectations upon us can reinforce the notion that we are not enough as we are. Over time, these words become part of the internal dialogue, etching deep grooves of self-doubt within our minds.

The demon's presence within our inner house intensifies as we navigate the complexities of adolescence. Social pressures, societal standards, and the turbulence of self-discovery further feed its expansion. It thrives on the uncertainty accompanying puberty, whispering doubts about our changing bodies, abilities, and desirability. Pursuing belonging and validation becomes a battleground where the demon fuels the fear of rejection and exclusion.

As we enter adulthood, Insecurity continues to evolve, intertwining with our sense of identity and self-worth. It seeks refuge in the memories of past failures and rejections, replaying these moments like a broken record. The comparison to others' achievements amplifies its voice, reinforcing the belief that our accomplishments are insignificant. Insecurity also feeds on the external pressures of societal expectations, the demands of a competitive world, and the relentless pursuit of perfection.

Insecurity extends to the very fabric of our thoughts, emotions, and behaviors. It taints our perceptions, distorting how we see ourselves and interpret the world. Its presence becomes particularly pronounced in moments of vulnerability—when we step outside our comfort zones, face criticism, or open ourselves to the possibility of failure. In these moments, the demon's whispers of inadequacy can be paralyzing, preventing us from fully embracing opportunities and realizing our potential.

The inner "demon" of insecurity is not a singular entity; it's a complex network of thoughts, beliefs, and emotions that weave together to form a pervasive presence within our inner house. It latches onto our self-doubts, fears, and past experiences, creating a self-perpetuating cycle that erodes our confidence and distorts our self-perception. It extends into various rooms of our mental mansion, impacting our relationships, decisions, and overall well-being.

Recognizing the birth and growth of insecurity is crucial in our journey toward healing and transformation. By understanding its origins and intricacies, we can unravel the threads of insecurity and rewrite the narratives that have held us captive for so long. Through self-compassion, introspection, and a commitment to change, we can free ourselves from the grips of this inner demon, paving the way for a life defined by authenticity, self-assurance, and the unwavering belief that we are worthy, just as we are.

Section 2: The Presence of Insecurity.

The insecurity within one's inner house gives rise to many distinct traits and behaviors that shape an individual's experiences, interactions, and worldview. These traits often stem from a deep-rooted sense of self-doubt, failure, and inadequacy, influencing a person's life.

One common trait among those harboring the inner "demon" of insecurity is a persistent sense of self-doubt. Individuals affected by insecurity question their abilities, accomplishments, and fundamental worthiness. This self-doubt can seep into various domains of their lives, from their professional endeavors to their relationships, often leading to hesitation, indecision, and a reluctance to take on new challenges.

Another prominent behavior associated with insecurity is an inclination towards perfectionism, as with other inner "demons." Those grappling with this situation often set excessively high standards for themselves, driven by the belief that they must prove their worth through flawless achievements. This pursuit of perfection can lead to chronic stress, anxiety, and a fear of failure, as any perceived shortcomings are magnified and internalized as reflections of their inadequacy.

Insecurity also tends to manifest in a tendency to seek external validation. These Individuals rely heavily on the approval and opinions of others to validate their self-worth. This can lead to a constant need for reassurance and affirmation, making them vulnerable to the fluctuations of others' views and hindering their ability to cultivate genuine self-esteem.

Avoidance behaviors are another hallmark of insecurity. To shield themselves from potential criticism or rejection, individuals may shy away from situations that trigger their feelings of inadequacy. This can result in missed opportunities for growth and personal development. Additionally, the fear of judgment can lead them to hide their true selves, preventing them from fully expressing their thoughts, emotions, and aspirations.

Social comparison is also a typical pattern among those grappling with insecurity. They may habitually compare themselves to others, often focusing on the perceived accomplishments and strengths of others while downplaying their achievements. This habit of comparison can foster feelings of envy, competition, and an ongoing sense of falling short, further fueling the demon's influence.

Insecurity can also influence an individual's relationships, often leading to difficulties in forming and maintaining connections. People affected by insecurity may struggle with trust issues, fearing that others will eventually uncover and reject their perceived flaws. This can lead to cycles of isolation as they grapple with a fear of vulnerability and the potential for rejection.

Furthermore, individuals contending with insecurity may engage in negative self-talk, constantly berating themselves with harsh criticism and judgments. This self-sabotaging dialogue reinforces the demon's influence, fostering a cycle of self-doubt and self-criticism that hinders personal growth and self-acceptance.

All these traits and behaviors associated with insecurity are varied and convoluted, forming a complex web that shapes how individuals perceive themselves and engage with the world. Recognizing these patterns is a crucial step in the journey toward healing and transformation, as it empowers individuals to challenge the grip of insecurity and cultivate a more compassionate, confident, and authentic sense of self.

Activity 6.1: Whispers of the Soul: Unveiling Insecurity.

Engage in a reflective activity that delves into the depths of your inner world to unveil the presence of the metaphorical inner demon of insecurity. This activity encourages you to listen to the whispers of your soul and uncover the subtle threads that this inner demon may weave.

Steps:

1. **Create a Sacred Space:** Find a quiet, comfortable space to sit without distractions. Light a candle or dim the lights to create a soothing atmosphere that encourages introspection.
2. **Breathe and Center:** Close your eyes and take a few deep breaths to center yourself. Inhale deeply, hold for a moment, and exhale slowly. Allow your body to relax and your mind to quiet.
3. **Connect with Your Intuition:** Place your hand over your heart and take a few more deep breaths. Focus on your heart center and imagine a warm light radiating from it. This is your intuitive space, where you can connect with the whispers of your soul.
4. **Ask the Question:** Write the question: "In what areas of my life do I feel uncertain or doubt myself?" Allow the question to resonate within you, inviting your subconscious mind to bring forth insights.

5. **Stream of Consciousness Writing:** Begin writing without censoring yourself. Let your thoughts flow freely onto the pages. Write down any thoughts, feelings, or memories that come to mind when contemplating the question. Don't worry about grammar or structure; this is a private space for your inner thoughts.

6. **Explore and Reflect:** After writing for a few minutes, read through your writing. Pay attention to any recurring themes, emotions, or patterns that emerge. Explore the connections between your thoughts and feelings and notice if they relate to feelings of insecurity.

7. **Metaphorical Exploration:** Imagine that your feelings of insecurity have a voice. If they were to speak, what would they say? Write down any messages, fears, or doubts that you feel are connected to this inner demon. Allow your intuition to guide your writing.

8. **Identify the Threads:** Look for common threads that link your insecurity to specific situations, relationships, or areas of your life. Are there particular triggers or circumstances that tend to activate these feelings? Write down these insights in your journal.

9. **Create an Affirmation:** Based on what you've uncovered, create a positive affirmation that directly addresses the feelings of insecurity you've identified. Craft a statement that embodies self-compassion, empowerment, and the intention to overcome these inner struggles.

10. **Visualize Transformation:** Close your eyes and visualize yourself standing in a place of strength and confidence. Envision yourself confidently facing the situations that trigger insecurity and feeling secure in your worth and capabilities.

11. **Gratitude and Closure:** Take a moment to express gratitude for the insights you've gained during this reflective journey. Close your journal and thank yourself for dedicating this time to self-discovery.

By entering this reflective expedition and listening to the whispers of your soul, you've engaged with the subtle currents of your inner world. Through your exploration, you've unveiled the presence of the metaphorical inner "demon" of insecurity, gaining insights into its influence on your thoughts and emotions. This activity is a meaningful step toward acknowledging, understanding, and eventually transforming this inner demon, paving the way for greater self-assurance and emotional well-being.

Activity 6.1: Whispers of the Soul: Unveiling Insecurity.

Healing activity 6.1: Conquering the Shackles of Insecurity.

Step into a realm of transformation with a self-therapeutic activity rooted in established psychotherapy techniques designed to dismantle the intricate web of insecurity and its accompanying traits. This empowering journey invites you to dive deep within, tapping into proven methods that resonate profoundly with your inner world and facilitate lasting change.

Steps:

1. **Intention Setting:** Find a tranquil space to focus your thoughts without distractions. Sit comfortably and close your eyes. Take a few deep breaths, inhaling through your nose and exhaling through your mouth. Set your intention for this activity: to confront and conquer the pervasive demon of insecurity.

2. **Exploration of Origins:** Go to the space provided and dedicate the page to exploring the origins of your insecurity. Begin by answering questions such as: When did you first notice feelings of insecurity? Were there specific events or experiences that triggered it? Be honest and open in your reflections.

3. **Root Cause Identification:** Delve deeper into your narrative and pinpoint your insecurity's root cause. Was it a childhood incident, a significant life change, or societal influences? Allow yourself to recall memories and emotions associated with these events.

4. **Unmasking Negative Beliefs:** Create a new journal page titled **"Negative Beliefs."** List the self-doubting thoughts and beliefs that stem from your insecurity. These might include

notions about your appearance, abilities, or worthiness. Acknowledge these beliefs without judgment.

5. **Reality Check:** On a separate page, challenge each negative belief with a reality check. Counteract these thoughts with evidence from your life that contradicts them. For instance, jot down cases in which you've succeeded or received praise if you believe you're not talented.

6. **Affirmation Transformation:** Turn to a fresh page labeled **"Empowering Affirmations."** Craft positive and empowering affirmations that counteract your negative beliefs. For instance, if your negative belief is about your appearance, your affirmation could be: "I am beautiful and unique as I am."

7. **Daily Affirmation Practice:** Incorporate your affirmations into your daily routine. Choose a specific time each day to recite these affirmations aloud or in your mind. This practice will gradually rewire your thought patterns, replacing self-doubt with self-assurance.

8. **Courageous Self-Compassion:** Take time to reflect on the journey you've embarked upon. Write a letter to your younger self, offering comfort, encouragement, and compassion. Share the wisdom you've gained and reassure your inner child that they are worthy and deserving of love.

9. **Visualization of Empowerment:** Close your eyes and visualize yourself confidently navigating situations that once triggered your insecurity. See yourself standing tall, radiating self-assuredness, and embracing your unique qualities without hesitation.

10. **Commitment to Transformation:** Conclude this activity by **affirming your commitment** to self-transformation. Write a pledge in your journal to continue dismantling the grip of insecurity and embracing your authentic self with unwavering confidence.

This self-therapeutic journey merges proven psychotherapy techniques with your inner strength, enabling you to break free from insecurity. By investigating its origins, challenging negative beliefs, and cultivating empowering affirmations, you're rewriting the script of your self-perception. As you continue this path of healing, remember that you're not alone—the resilience within you is a force to be reckoned with. Through consistent practice, self-compassion, and the determination to foster change, you're opening the door to a life guided by self-assurance, acceptance, and an unshakable belief in your inherent worthiness.

Healing activity 6.1: Conquering the Shackles of Insecurity.

Healing tool 6.2: Soul Retrieving: Unveiling the inner Radiance.

Delve into the realms of Soul retrieval and memory healing with an imaginative and transformative self-therapeutic activity that guides you on a captivating journey of self-discovery. This unique approach will help you overcome insecurity by unraveling its grip and embracing your inner radiance.

Materials Needed:

- Small mirror
- A quiet and comfortable space
- Journal or notebook
- Pen or pencil
- Your favorite calming scent (essential oil, incense, etc.)
- Soft and soothing background music (optional)

Steps:

1. **Setting the Sacred Space:** Create a tranquil atmosphere by dimming the lights and infusing the air with your chosen calming scent. Play soft background music if desired, letting it envelop you in a soothing ambiance.
2. **Mirror Connection:** Hold the small mirror in your hands, feeling its energy and potential. Acknowledge that the mirror reflects not only your external appearance but also your inner essence and potential. Gaze into the mirror's reflection, acknowledging any emotions that arise.
3. **Inviting Inner Wisdom:** Close your eyes and take a few deep breaths. Imagine standing at the entrance of a serene garden in your mind. This garden represents your inner world, brimming with memories and emotions. As you step into this garden, envision a tranquil pond.

4. **Memory Ripples:** *Imagine gently dropping a pebble into the pond's still waters. Watch as the ripples spread across the surface, representing the memories and experiences tied to your insecurities. Let the waves guide you towards a memory that holds the essence of your insecurity.*

5. **Soulful Exploration:** *With the memory in mind, sit comfortably with your journal and pen. Begin writing a letter to your younger self, addressing the feelings of insecurity from your chosen memory. Offer the compassion and wisdom you possess now, encouraging your younger self to release the burden.*

6. **Mirror Dialogue:** *Return to the mirror, holding it before you. Gaze into your eyes and allow yourself to speak aloud or silently. Share the insights and healing messages you've written in the letter with the reflection of your eyes. Feel the connection between your present self and your younger self.*

7. **Reframing Reflection:** *Imagine the mirror's reflection transforming into a vibrant, radiant version of yourself—a visual representation of your inner radiance. Visualize the light dispelling the shadows of insecurity and illuminating your true worthiness.*

8. **Symbol of Empowerment:** *Find a small object symbolizing your newfound empowerment and self-confidence. This could be a crystal, a miniature artwork, or any item that resonates with you. Please place it in your journal or beside the mirror as a reminder of your journey.*

9. **Journal Reflection:** *In your journal, record your experiences, insights, and any messages you received during the mirror dialogue. Reflect on how the memory's energy has shifted and how your perspective on the memory has transformed.*

10. **Daily Ritual:** *Incorporate a brief daily ritual where you gaze into the mirror and affirm your self-worth. With each reflection, acknowledge your progress and reiterate your commitment to embracing your inner radiance.*

11. **Garden Visualization:** *Regularly revisit the garden within your mind. Envision the serene, clear, vibrant pond, reflecting your inner*

radiance. As you drop pebbles into the pond, witness the ripples representing your growing self-assurance.

12. **Culminating Celebration:** Conclude this activity by celebrating your journey of self-discovery. Light a candle, and express gratitude for the insights and healing you've gained. As the flame flickers, acknowledge that you are lighting the way toward a life infused with self-confidence and inner radiance.

This imaginative journey into the realms of Soul Retrieving and memory healing uncovers the hidden treasures of your self-worth, shattering the grip of insecurity. You are writing a new narrative of self-assurance and empowerment by engaging with your reflection, revisiting the past, and embracing your inner radiance. As you continue this transformative practice, remember that the mirror reflects not only your external form but also the resilience and beauty of your soul. Embrace your journey with grace and curiosity, knowing each step leads you closer to a life enriched by your innate radiance and unwavering self-belief.

Personal Note:

As we navigate life's complexities, we inevitably encounter in-security in our minds and hearts. It's essential to take a moment to reflect on our progress in conquering these inner "demons" and to appreciate the strength and radiance that emanate from within us despite any shadows we may face.

Dear reader, you've demonstrated exceptional courage in con-fronting the subtle murmurs of self-doubt that once plagued you. Armed with self-compassion and self-awareness, you've emerged as a true warrior. It's no small feat to unravel the complexities of insecurities that once held you captive, to examine their origins, and to peel away the layers of negative self-talk that once obscured your brilliance. In this process, you've discovered the power of your own story. By shining a light on the origins of your insecurities, you've taken away their ability to define you. You've freed yourself from the destructive comparison cycle and embraced your unique qualities. Acknowledging your insecurities has shifted the narrative from one of vulnerability to one of empowerment.

CHAPTER 7: TRAUMA: CONFRONTING THE GREATEST DEMON.

As we venture into the heart of our journey, we approach a colossal and dirtiest labyrinth—the realm of trauma. Recognized as the mightiest metaphorical "demon," trauma holds the power to shape our very existence, casting shadows on every corner of our mental house and beyond. This chapter is not mere; it's a portal into a universe where pain, healing, and resilience intertwine, a vast realm that could warrant its book.

Trauma, the titan among inner "demons," demands our unwavering attention and respect. Its impact reaches beyond individual experiences, echoing across generations and weaving its threads into the fabric of our thoughts, emotions, and behaviors. Its touch can be agonizingly painful, often lurking beneath the surface, yet its influence is undeniable.

Here, we go on a profound exploration, navigating through the valleys of the most common traumas that many of us carry. We recognize that this journey will take time and effort. Trauma doesn't yield easy answers or quick fixes. It's a complex tapestry woven from experiences we'd rather forget and emotions that threaten to overwhelm us.

We acknowledge that this chapter will be long, at times painful, but profoundly important. Our commitment to confronting this formidable "demon" is born from the understanding that its shackles keep us from our highest potential. Through compassion, understanding, and the strength to face our past, we aim to unravel the tightly woven threads of trauma's influence.

The traumas we'll explore span a broad spectrum, from early childhood experiences to adult life events. We'll delve into the labyrinth of neglect, abuse, loss, and violence—each a distinct shade of pain, yet interconnected by the common thread of their aftermath. As we shed light on the darkness, we aim to unveil the traumas themselves and ignite the path toward healing.

It's crucial to remember that this journey is a profound act of self-compassion. By entering this space, you're acknowledging the strength it takes to confront your innermost pain. While the road ahead may be arduous, it's also paved with the potential for liberation. The demons that haunt us through trauma can be transformed into catalysts for growth, resilience, and profound self-discovery.

As we journey into the depths of trauma, remember, as I have written repeatedly, that you're not alone in this exploration. Together, we'll navigate the labyrinth, shining light on the wounds that have festered in darkness for far too long. With courage as our guide, we're poised to uncover the dormant power within us, transforming pain into empowerment and reclaiming the light that trauma sought to extinguish.

Section 1: Neglect: The Silent Wound of Trauma.

In the convoluted road of human experiences, neglect is a haunting shadow—one of the threads contributing to the complex inner "demon" of trauma. Often overshadowed by more overt forms of abuse, neglect is the silent wound that leaves its mark on the psyche, shaping perceptions, emotions, and the very sense of self. It's a profound betrayal of the fundamental human need for care, leaving scars that may be invisible to the eye yet profoundly etched within the soul.

Neglect takes many forms, but at its core, it's an absence—a void where there should have been a presence, where nurturing and protection were expected but never materialized. It's the absence of a parent's comforting embrace, a consistent support system, and emotional attunement. It can be a physical absence, an emotional absence, or a combination of both, each variation leaving its unique imprint on the individual's internal landscape.

Children who endure neglect often navigate a lonely terrain where their emotional needs go unmet, their cries for attention unheard. In a world where they should have found safety and validation, they are left adrift, struggling to make sense of their worth without affirmation. The neglect trauma can manifest in many ways, echoing throughout life. It might be reflected in an adult's difficulty forming and maintaining healthy relationships, a persistent belief in one's inadequacy, or even a propensity to self-sabotage due to deeply ingrained feelings of unworthiness.

The aftermath of neglect often intertwines with a profound sense of shame—the belief that they somehow did not deserve love and care. This self-perception becomes a lens through which the world is viewed, impacting the ability to trust, connect, and find solace in relationships. The scars of neglect can also manifest in the form of perfectionism, as individuals strive to prove their worthiness by excelling in various domains, hoping that achievements will fill the void left by neglect.

Healing from neglect within the realm of trauma requires a delicate balance of self-compassion and a willingness to confront the pain head-on. It involves recognizing that the absence of care was not a reflection of the individual's inherent value but rather a failure on the caregiver's part. The healing journey may involve re-parenting oneself and learning to provide the care and nurturing lacking in earlier years.

In exploring neglect as a facet of trauma, we shed light on this silent wound's profound impact on an individual's life trajectory. It's an invitation to understand the complexity of trauma, to hold space for the pain of those whose wounds are less visible but no less significant. By acknowledging the scars of neglect and giving voice to the silent pain, we step toward breaking the chains of trauma's influence, reclaiming a sense of agency, and fostering a path toward healing, connection, and self-acceptance.

Section 1.2: Traits of Neglect's Impact.

In human psychology, the trauma of neglect creates traits and behaviors with profound significance. This tyrant, born from the deprivation of essential emotional nourishment, shapes the lens through which individuals perceive themselves, relationships, and the world around them. Its influence is far-reaching in our behaviors, thoughts, and emotions.

1. **Hyper-vigilance and Distrust**: The trauma of neglect fosters an acute awareness of potential abandonment. This awareness often translates into a heightened vigilance—an underlying belief that one must be ever watchful for signs

of rejection. This hyper-vigilance can lead to difficulty in fully trusting others, always anticipating when the perceived safety of connection will shatter.

2. **Self-Doubt and Inadequacy**: The trauma of neglect plants the seeds of self-doubt and inadequacy deep within. Individuals who have experienced neglect often struggle with an intrinsic belief that they are unworthy of love and attention. This belief may manifest as constant self-criticism, undeserving of success, or downplaying one's achievements to avoid drawing attention.

3. **Avoidance of Intimacy**: The trauma of neglect can lead to avoiding intimate relationships. The fear of potential rejection or emotional pain becomes a powerful deterrent, causing individuals to distance themselves from situations that may evoke vulnerability. This avoidance can manifest in both romantic relationships and friendships.

4. **Perfectionism**: The trauma of neglect can drive individuals to seek external validation to compensate for the internal void left by neglect. This quest for validation may lead to perfectionism—a relentless pursuit of flawlessness to gain approval and affirmation from others.

5. **Fear of Abandonment**: The trauma of neglect casts a shadow of fear over the possibility of abandonment, perpetually haunting individuals' interactions. This fear can lead to clinginess in relationships, an overwhelming need for constant reassurance, or an inability to assert one's needs for fear of pushing others away.

6. **Difficulty Expressing Needs**: The trauma of neglect often hinders the development of healthy communication skills, particularly in expressing one's needs. Individuals who have experienced neglect may struggle to articulate their emotions and requirements, fearing rejection or dismissal.

7. **Tendency to Self-Isolate**: The trauma of neglect can create a pattern of withdrawing from others as a protective measure.

Individuals may choose solitude to avoid the potential pain of rejection or disappointment, unintentionally exacerbating feelings of loneliness.

8. **Submissive or People-Pleasing Behaviors**: The trauma of neglect can manifest in behaviors aimed at avoiding conflict and seeking approval. Individuals might engage in people-pleasing behaviors, subordinating their needs and desires to maintain the illusion of connection and acceptance.

9. **Difficulty Setting Boundaries**: The trauma of neglect can undermine one's ability to set and enforce healthy boundaries. A fear of abandonment may lead individuals to compromise their boundaries, making it challenging to protect their emotional well-being.

10. **Feelings of Loneliness**: The trauma of neglect's legacy often includes an enduring sense of loneliness. This loneliness isn't solely about physical solitude; it's the feeling of being emotionally isolated and disconnected from others on a deeper level.

As these traits and behaviors intertwine, they shape the complex portrait of someone who has navigated the tumultuous waters of neglect's trauma. Recognizing these traits are not inherent flaws; responses to a profound experience are crucial. Understanding and addressing the impact of neglect trauma requires a compassionate journey of self-discovery, self-compassion, and intentional healing.

By illuminating these traits and behaviors, we can peel back the layers that the trauma of neglect has shaped. Through this understanding, we pave the way for a transformative process that empowers individuals to rewrite the narrative, forge healthy connections, and embark on a journey of self-compassion, self-worth, and healing.

Healing tool 7.1 Reclaiming Wholeness - Healing from the Trauma of Neglect.

Healing from the profound trauma of neglect requires a deeply personal journey that beckons you to explore your inner world with compassion and resilience. This self-guided activity is your companion on this transformative path, utilizing advanced psychotherapy techniques to help you navigate the intricate layers of neglect's impact. Through this exploration, you can rewrite the narrative that neglect has woven into your life and embrace the profound healing that comes with it.

Instructions:

1. **Creating a Haven:** Begin by seeking a quiet, comfortable space to immerse yourself in this self-healing experience. Gently close your eyes and take a few deep breaths, allowing your body and mind to settle into a state of calm presence.
2. **A Journey Back in Time:** Visualize yourself as the child you once were, standing at the threshold of the past where the seeds of neglect were sown. Transport yourself to the specific setting where you first encountered the weight of neglect— whether it's the echoing halls of your childhood home, the classroom where your voice remained unheard, or any place that holds resonance.
3. **Guided Imagery: The Healing Light:** Envision a gentle, soothing light surrounding your younger self—a light that signifies the love, warmth, and protection you deserve. Let this light symbolize the nurturing care that may have been absent during those moments. Feel this light embrace your inner child, wrapping them in an aura of healing.
4. **Conversing with Your Inner Child:** Approach your younger self within this visualization. Imagine sitting down with this innocent and vulnerable version of you. Engage in a heartfelt

conversation where you listen as intently as you speak. Ask your inner child how they feel, what they need, and what they've always wanted to express.

5. **Validation and Empathy:** As you converse with your inner child, validate their feelings without judgment. Offer empathy and understanding, acknowledging the pain they endured. Share words of compassion and reassurance, assuring your younger self that their emotions are valid and worthy of acknowledgment.

6. **Becoming Your Nurturing Guardian:** Step into the role of the adult you needed during that time—a guardian who offers unwavering support, guidance, and unconditional love. Speak to your inner child with the wisdom you've gained through life's journey. Offer words of encouragement, promising to protect and cherish them moving forward.

7. **Healing Gestures of Release:** Visualize a powerful symbolic act of release. This could be represented by releasing a balloon into the sky and watching it carry away the burdens of the past. As you do so, affirm that you are liberating yourself from the weight of neglect's impact on your life.

8. **Crafting Your Inner Sanctuary:** Envision an inner sanctuary within your mind—a sanctuary of solace, love, and acceptance. Create this sanctuary in intricate detail, imagining the soothing elements that make it a safe haven. Whether it's a peaceful garden, a tranquil beach, or a serene forest clearing, this sanctuary is your retreat.

9. **Affirmation and Embrace:** Conclude the activity with a personal affirmation that resonates deeply with you. This affirmation reaffirms your worthiness and strength. Please take a few moments to let this affirmation permeate your being, embracing the healing energy it brings.

10. **Journaling Your Journey:** After completing the activity, sit down with your journal and capture your thoughts, feelings, and insights. Reflect on the profound experience of

connecting with your inner child and embarking on this healing journey. Journaling solidifies your discoveries and anchors your commitment to self-healing.

This self-guided activity is a testament to your courage and determination to heal from the trauma of neglect. By forging a compassionate connection with your inner child, you embark on a journey of profound transformation. Remember that healing is a process, and with each step you take, you are rewriting the narrative of your past, embracing your intrinsic worth, and paving the way for a future defined by resilience, self-compassion, and genuine self-love.

Journaling Your Journey:

Section 2: Ripping of the Covering of Abuse.

As we explore the complexities of human life, we uncover various experiences, some bright and others dark, that shape who we are. Continuing our journey into the topic of trauma, we now focus on a powerful "demon" that leaves a long-lasting and haunting impact—abuse. This section encourages us to dive deep into the heart of this harmful force that causes deep soul wounds to reverberate through our lives.

The origins of suffering within the context of abuse often emerge from the interweaving dynamics of power and vulnerability. It takes root when those intended as protectors turn into tormentors, shattering trust and tarnishing the innocence of youth with the cruelty of others. Whether taking on the form of physical violence, emotional manipulation, or insidious coercion, abuse weaves a complex tapestry of agony.

The repercussions of abuse extend beyond visible scars; they infiltrate the very essence of our being. Unraveling threads of thought, emotion, and relationships leaves fragments of emotions and distorted perceptions behind. Post-abuse, individuals grapple with buried memories while striving to carve a semblance of normalcy within a fragmented reality.

Survivors of abuse often wrestle with a sense of fractured selfhood. Wounds inflicted distort their identity, leading to questioning of self-worth and marring perceptions of personal agency. The aftermath burdens survivors with guilt erroneously attributed to them, as scars deeply etch into their psyche, both evident and concealed.

Ripples of abuse extend beyond individuals, impacting the bonds that connect us. Trust, once a steadfast bridge, becomes fragile and susceptible to collapse. Intimacy becomes a battleground between yearning for connection and fear of vulnerability. Survivors may contend with emotional withdrawal or aggression as they navigate the remnants of pain.

Healing from abuse trauma isn't a linear process; it's a courageous journey demanding unwavering self-compassion. It commences with acknowledging the darkness, confronting pain, and navigating the intricate maze of emotions. This journey is marked by resolute steps, valleys of despair, and peaks of empowerment— an expedition toward rewriting narratives, reclaiming self-worth, and acknowledging the right to a life emancipated from the grip of the past.

As we plunge into the repercussions of abuse's impact, let us honor survivors' resilience. The scars that remain are testaments to the strength that emerges from adversity. Healing evolves, a continual transformation where steps toward acknowledgment, recovery, and release represent steps toward liberation.

Our exploration into the aftermath of abuse urges us to confront shadows, confront pain head-on, and witness the potential for metamorphosis. By acknowledging the pain and reclaiming stories, we inch closer to transforming the inner "demon" of abuse into a catalyst for growth. As we navigate these depths, let's recall our inherent ability to heal, rebuild, and thrive.

Activity 7.2: Recognizing Abused.

Trauma, especially abuse, can manifest in complex ways within our lives. This activity will help you explore your experiences and emotions, identify potential signs of abuse trauma, and understand how it might affect you. It's a crucial step toward healing and seeking the support you may need.

Instructions:

1. **Self-Reflection:** Find a peaceful place to be alone with your thoughts. Take a few deep breaths to center yourself.
2. **Journaling Your Feelings:** Open your journal and write your feelings without judgment. Allow your emotions to flow freely onto the pages. Consider moments that have felt particularly challenging, distressing, or uncomfortable.
3. **Exploring Possible Triggers:** Review your journal entries and identify recurring themes, situations, or memories that evoke strong emotional reactions. These situations might cause anxiety, sadness, anger, or fear.
4. **Mapping Emotions:** Create a visual representation of your emotions. Draw a simple chart with emotions along one axis (e.g., anger, fear, sadness) and situations/events along the other (e.g., arguments with certain people, specific places, particular memories).
5. **Patterns and Connections:** Examine your chart. Notice if there are any patterns or connections between specific situations/events and the emotions you've been experiencing. Are there particular triggers that consistently evoke strong reactions?
6. **Physical Sensations:** Reflect on any physical sensations you experience when these emotions arise. Note if there are any physical manifestations like tension, rapid heartbeat, shallow breathing, etc.
7. **Comparing Past and Present:** Think about how your emotional reactions and physical sensations compare to your experiences in

the past. Have you encountered similar emotions or feelings before, perhaps during earlier distressing situations?

8. **Identifying Abuse Trauma:** If you notice a significant alignment between past distressing situations and your current emotional and physical responses, this could indicate unresolved trauma, possibly stemming from abuse.

Completing this activity requires courage and self-awareness. It's important to remember that self-identification is a significant step in your healing journey. If you've identified signs of abuse trauma, know you're not alone, and support is available. If you've found that your emotions are challenging to manage, seeking the guidance of a mental health professional can provide you with tools to heal and thrive.

Activity 7.1: Recognizing Abused.

Healing tool 7.1 Healing from Abuse Trauma: A Self-Therapy Journey.

Healing from abuse trauma is a profound journey that requires self-compassion, courage, and the application of evidence-based psychotherapy techniques. This self-therapy guide empowers you with tools rooted in psychological research to navigate the complexities of abuse trauma and embark on a path of healing and transformation.

Instructions:

1. **Grounding and Awareness:**

   - Find a comfortable space where you can focus without distractions.
   - Close your eyes and take a few deep breaths. As you inhale, imagine drawing in healing energy. As you exhale, release tension and negativity.
   - Gradually bring your awareness to your surroundings. Notice the sensation of your body against a surface and the sounds around you. This practice grounds you in the present moment, helping to alleviate anxiety and stress.

1. **Journaling Your Story:**

   - Open your journal or the space provided and dedicate a section to your healing journey.
   - Begin by writing your story. Please include details of your abusive experiences, the emotions they stirred, and how they've impacted your life. Let your feelings flow freely onto the pages.

1. **Identifying Triggers:**

- *Review your journal entries and identify triggers—situations, places, or people that evoke strong emotional responses or discomfort.*
- *Note these triggers and the emotions associated with them. This step enhances self-awareness and provides insight into the root causes of your emotional reactions.*

1. **Cognitive Restructuring:**

- *Identify negative thought patterns that arise from triggers. Challenge each negative thought by asking questions like, "Is this thought based on facts or assumptions?" and "What evidence supports or contradicts this thought?"*
- *Replace distorted thoughts with more balanced and realistic alternatives. This technique gradually shifts your perspective and diminishes the power of negative beliefs.*

1. **Emotional Regulation:**

- *Use emotional regulation techniques like deep breathing, progressive muscle relaxation, and mindfulness meditation. Practice these regularly to manage intense emotions triggered by memories of abuse.*

1. **Inner Child Healing:**

- *Visualize yourself as a child experiencing the abuse. Connect with the emotions you felt at that time. Imagine stepping into the scene as your present self, offering comfort, protection, and support to your younger self.*

1. **Self-Compassion Practice:**

- *Cultivate self-compassion by treating yourself with the same kindness and understanding you'd offer a friend. Practice self-compassion meditation and write self-compassionate letters to yourself in moments of pain.*

1. *Gradual Exposure:*

• *Create a hierarchy of situations or memories related to the abuse, ranging from least triggering to most triggering. Gradually expose yourself to these situations controlled and safely, building resilience over time.*

Remember that healing from abuse trauma is a nonlinear process that requires time, patience, and dedication. This self-therapy guide equips you with practical techniques rooted in psychological research. However, if your trauma is severe or interfering with your daily life, seeking professional help is crucial for comprehensive healing. You deserve to reclaim your life, rewrite your story, and embrace a future of empowerment, resilience, and newfound strength.

Healing tool 7.1 Healing from Abuse Trauma: A Self-Therapy Journey.

Healing tool 7.2 Reclaiming Wholeness after Abuse Trauma.

Soul Retrieving is a transformative self-therapy technique rooted in ancient wisdom and supported by contemporary psychology. This method draws upon retrieving fragmented parts of the self that may have been lost or dissociated due to trauma. By engaging in this practice, you can embark on a profound journey of healing from abuse trauma and reclaim the parts of yourself that have been impacted.

Instructions:

1. **Preparation:**

- *Find a quiet space where you can be alone and undisturbed.*
- *Sit or lie comfortably, allowing yourself to feel grounded and relaxed.*

1. **Establishing Intention:**

- *Close your eyes and take a few deep breaths. With each inhale, imagine drawing in healing energy. With each exhale, release tension and negativity.*
- *Set a clear intention for your Soul Retrieving journey. It could be something like, "I intend to reclaim the parts of myself that have been lost to abuse trauma."*

1. **Inner Sanctuary Visualization:**

- *Begin by imagining yourself in a safe and serene place. This is your inner sanctuary—where you can connect with your higher self and begin the retrieval process.*

1. **Meeting Your Inner Guide:**

- *Visualize a wise and compassionate guide within your inner sanctuary. This guide represents your higher self or a symbol of divine wisdom.*

1. **Seeking the Lost Aspects:**

- *Express your intention to your inner guide and ask for assistance in retrieving the parts of yourself that were fragmented due to abuse.*
- *Trust that your guide will lead you to the aspects of yourself that need healing and integration.*

1. **Visualization of Retrieval:**

- *Imagine your guide leading you through different landscapes or scenes. You may encounter aspects of yourself that feel wounded, hurt, or dissociated in each stage.*
- *Approach each aspect with empathy and love. Engage in conversations, offering comfort, validation, and reassurance.*

1. **Integration and Healing:**

- *As you connect with each fragmented aspect, visualize it merging into your being. Feel the energy of wholeness and healing as you integrate these parts.*

1. **Reflection and Journaling:**

- *After the visualization, take some time to reflect on your experience. What aspects of yourself did you encounter? What emotions or sensations arose during the process?*
- *Write down your reflections in your journal. This process helps solidify the healing work you've done.*

1. **Revisit and Repeat:**

- *Soul Retrieving is not a one-time event. You can revisit this practice whenever you need to heal and integrate further.*
- *Each time you engage in this practice, you may encounter different aspects and experiences, deepening your healing journey.*

Soul Retrieving is a profound self-therapy technique that allows you to reclaim the parts of yourself affected by abuse trauma. This practice combines ancient wisdom with modern psychological understanding, offering a holistic approach to healing. Remember that healing from abuse trauma is a gradual process, and Soul Retrieving can be a valuable tool to support your journey toward wholeness and empowerment. If your trauma is severe or overwhelming, professional help is recommended to ensure comprehensive healing and support.

Healing tool 7.2 Reclaiming Wholeness after Abuse Trauma.

Section 3: Loss, losing, and lost.

Humans often experience a deep and haunting ache known as the trauma of loss. This emotion profoundly impacts us and resonates, bringing back memories of what once was. We feel this emotion when we say goodbye to something or someone cherished and are left with a void. It weaves its threads deep into the fabric of our souls and echoes through the corridors of our inner house.

Originating from the heart's profound connection, the trauma of loss unfolds as a response to the disruption of that connection. It is born from the interplay between attachment and separation, reminding us of the impermanence that shadows all existence. This emotion dwells in moments of departure—whether it be the passing of a loved one, the end of a relationship, or the fading of a significant chapter in life. In these moments, the trauma of loss emerges as a silent witness to the ebb and flow of life's transitions.

The experience of loss, with its unique texture and depth, paints a complexity of emotions. Grief, a faithful companion to loss, encompasses an array of emotions—sorrow, longing, anger, and even confusion. It is an emotional landscape marked by upheaval as the familiar gives way to the unfamiliar. The trauma of loss beckons us to grapple with the profound absence as we navigate the void left behind by what once was.

The trauma of loss extends its reach into the realm of identity, influencing how we perceive ourselves and our place in the world. It can evoke questions of purpose and meaning, prompting introspection into the nature of existence itself. In the wake of loss, individuals often experience a reevaluation of their values, priorities, and aspirations—a journey toward understanding their resilience in the face of life's fluctuations.

Various coping and defense mechanisms come into play within the trauma of loss. Denial, for instance, can be a shield against the harsh reality of absence, offering temporary refuge from the pain. Bargaining may arise as individuals attempt to negotiate with fate to reverse the irrevocable. Anguish may be expressed through anger, a response to the injustice perceived in the departure. While these mechanisms serve as emotional armor, they also reflect the intricacies of our human nature as we grapple with the indelible impact of loss.

The trauma of loss resonates through every aspect of human relationships, influencing how we engage with others. It can deepen our empathy, fostering a shared understanding of the fragility of existence. Simultaneously, it may lead to withdrawal as individuals attempt to shield themselves from the potential pain of future losses. These shifts, profound in their implications, reflect the intricate dance between vulnerability and resilience that the trauma of loss demands.

In the journey of healing from the trauma of loss, acknowledging the depth of emotion becomes a pivotal step. As we work on grief, permitting ourselves to experience the range of emerging emotions is an act of self-compassion. Sharing our stories and experiences can also foster connection, reminding us that we are not alone in our pain.

Reclaiming a sense of meaning and continuity in the aftermath of loss requires a delicate dance between honoring the past and embracing the present. Rituals, creative expression, and commemorations can serve as bridges between what was and what is, allowing us to acknowledge the significance of what has departed while finding solace in the beauty of the present moment.

Ultimately, the trauma of loss, while marked by its capacity to wound, also holds the potential to foster growth and transformation. In navigating its depths, we discover reservoirs of strength we never knew existed within us. The journey through grief becomes a testament to the human spirit's ability to transcend adversity and emerge on the other side, carrying the lessons of loss as precious gems of wisdom.

Section 3.1 Traits and behaviors of the inner "demon" of loss.

The effects of trauma caused by loss show up in various ways, impacting how a person feels and interacts with the world. When someone experiences loss, like the death of a loved one, a breakup, or a significant life change, it leaves a deep mark on their mind and can significantly affect their thoughts, emotions, and behavior. One common trait among individuals grappling with the trauma of loss is a pervasive sense of emptiness. This hollowness stems from the void left by the departure of a person, place, or thing that held significant meaning. This emotional void often accompanies a feeling of numbness, where the intensity of emotions is blunted as a defense mechanism against overwhelming pain. Individuals may describe this sensation as if a part of them has been taken away, leaving a persistent ache that colors their everyday experiences.

Grief, an intrinsic response to loss, often permeates the lives of those with trauma. This grief can take various forms, including sadness, anger, guilt, and confusion. The emotional intensity of grief can be overwhelming, leading to unpredictable mood shifts and affecting daily functioning. Individuals may oscillate between moments of deep sorrow and fleeting glimpses of hope.

A heightened sense of vulnerability is another characteristic trait of those who have experienced the trauma of loss. The sudden and unexpected nature of many losses shatters the illusion of control over one's life. This vulnerability can lead to heightened anxiety as individuals grapple with the realization that life can change instantly. This state of hyper-awareness may prompt individuals to adopt cautious behaviors or avoid situations that could trigger feelings of vulnerability.

Individuals affected by loss trauma may also experience difficulties in forming or maintaining relationships. The fear of attachment, only to experience the pain of separation again, can lead to emotional withdrawal and guardedness. Trust issues may arise as individuals struggle to open themselves up to new connections for fear of future loss. These behaviors can inadvertently isolate individuals, creating a self-perpetuating cycle of loneliness and emotional distance.

Changes in coping mechanisms are another telltale sign of trauma resulting from loss. Some individuals may turn to avoidant behaviors, attempting to numb the pain through substances, distractions, or other unhealthy habits. On the other hand, others might become hyper-focused on their grief, unable to move beyond the overwhelming emotions. Coping strategies can vary greatly and are often influenced by cultural norms, personal upbringing, and past experiences with loss.

The trauma of loss can also influence an individual's perception of time and future orientation. For some, the future may appear uncertain and bleak, leading to feelings of hopelessness. For others, the passage of time can evoke anxiety, as it signifies moving further away from the departed entity. This temporal distortion can affect a person's ability to set goals, plan, or envision a life beyond the trauma.

Sleep disturbances and changes in daily routines are common behavioral expressions of loss trauma. The emotional turmoil accompanying grief can disrupt sleep patterns, leading to insomnia, nightmares, or oversleeping. Daily routines may also become disrupted as individuals grapple with the impact of their loss on their sense of normalcy. These changes can further exacerbate feelings of disorientation and instability.

Individuals challenging the trauma of loss often experience a complicated relationship with memories. On one hand, cherished memories can serve as a source of comfort, allowing individuals to maintain a connection with what was lost. On the other hand, memories can trigger intense emotions and pain, leading to avoidance or even intrusive thoughts. This ambivalence towards memories can create a complex dance between seeking solace and avoiding emotional triggers.

The traits and behaviors exhibited by individuals with the trauma of loss are a testament to the profound impact that loss can have on the human psyche. From the pervasive emptiness and intense grief to the altered coping mechanisms and relationship changes, the aftermath of loss shapes how individuals perceive themselves, others, and the world around them. Acknowledging and addressing these traits and behaviors through support, therapy, and self-compassion is essential for navigating the journey toward healing and reclaiming a sense of wholeness after the shattering experience of loss.

Healing tool 7.3 Resilience through Renewal.

The path to healing from loss trauma is a courageous and transformative path that requires embracing pain, fostering resilience, and ultimately renewing the sense of self. This self-guided psychotherapy program draws from evidence-based practices to empower individuals to navigate the complexities of loss, promoting healing and growth.

Step 1: Acknowledging the Pain.

Begin by creating a safe and reflective space. Allow yourself to sit with your emotions and thoughts without judgment. Recognize the depth of your pain and grief. Engage in journaling to express your feelings, allowing the words to flow without self-censorship. This step encourages emotional release and lays the foundation for healing.

Step 2: Cultivating Self-Compassion.

Embrace self-compassion as a powerful tool for healing. Engage in daily mindfulness exercises, such as meditation or deep breathing. When negative self-talk arises, counter it with self-affirmations. Practice treating yourself with the kindness and understanding you would offer a dear friend.

Step 3: Exploring Memories and Emotions.

Create a "Memory Journal." Recall positive memories of the person, place, or thing you've lost. Reflect on the emotions these memories evoke. Allow yourself to grieve fully, acknowledging both the joy and pain of these moments. This process helps you honor your experiences and feelings.

Step 4: Reconstructing the Narrative.

Craft a narrative that encapsulates your journey through loss. Highlight your strengths, resilience, and growth. Share this narrative with a trusted friend or therapist. This step promotes a sense of agency and authorship over your story, allowing you to transform pain into purpose.

Step 5: Seeking Social Support.

Engage in meaningful connections with friends, family, or support groups. Share your experiences and feelings openly. Listen to others' stories and offer empathy. Connecting with others who understand and validate your emotions can provide a sense of belonging and alleviate isolation.

Step 6: Practicing Self-Care.

Prioritize self-care by engaging in activities that nurture your physical, emotional, and mental well-being. Establish a routine that includes regular exercise, a balanced diet, and sufficient sleep. Engage in creative outlets, such as art or music, to channel your emotions constructively—review volume 1.

Step 7: Imagery Rescripting.

Utilize imagery rescripting, an evidence-based technique, to address distressing memories. Imagine yourself in the traumatic event, then gently rewrite the scenario with a positive outcome. This practice can help diminish the emotional charge associated with the memory.

Step 8: Setting Goals and Future Focus.

Articulate short-term and long-term goals for your healing journey. Focus on aspects that bring you joy and fulfillment. Set incremental steps toward these goals, celebrating each achievement along the way. This forward-looking approach fosters hope and empowerment.

Step 9: Gratitude Practice.

Incorporate a daily gratitude practice into your routine. Each day, reflect on three things you're grateful for. This practice shifts your focus from loss to the positive aspects of your life, promoting a more balanced perspective.

Step 10: Closure Ritual.

Design a closure ritual that symbolizes your healing journey. This could involve creating an art piece, writing a letter, or planting a tree in memory. Engage in this ritual mindfully, infusing it with your intentions for healing and renewal.

This self-guided psychotherapy tool empowers individuals to confront loss trauma with resilience and purpose. By embracing pain, cultivating self-compassion, and engaging in evidence-based practices, you can navigate the complex landscape of grief and emerge on the other side with a renewed sense of self, purpose, and inner strength. Remember that healing is a gradual process, and your commitment to self-care and growth will guide you toward a brighter, more empowered future.

Healing tool 7.4 Reclaiming Wholeness: A Soul-Retrieving Approach to Overcome Loss Trauma.

The path to healing from loss trauma requires deeply exploring the self, drawing upon the ancient wisdom of soul-retrieving practices. By engaging in this science-based self-therapy, you embark on a transformative journey to reclaim the fragmented aspects of your being and restore a sense of wholeness.

Step 1: Creating a Sacred Space.

Set the intention for your healing process by creating a dedicated space. This space serves as a sanctuary to engage in introspection and soul-retrieving practices. Light a candle, play soothing music, or surround yourself with objects that evoke a sense of peace.

Step 2: Communing with Your Inner Self.

Engage in mindfulness meditation (review chapter 7 of volume 1) to cultivate a deeper connection with your inner self. In this state of heightened awareness, acknowledge your emotions without judgment. This practice helps you establish a compassionate foundation for the journey ahead.

Step 3: Guided Imagery.

Utilize guided imagery to journey within. Envision yourself in a serene natural setting like a forest or meadow. As you explore this inner landscape, seek out fragments of your soul that have been scattered by loss trauma. Gently invite these fragments to return to you.

Step 4: Symbolic Gathering.

Select symbolic objects that represent the different aspects of your being. Arrange these objects in a way that feels harmonious and balanced. As you place each object, silently invite the corresponding element of your soul to rejoin you, contributing to your sense of wholeness.

Step 5: Soul Dialogue.

Initiate a dialogue with the retrieved fragments of your soul. Through writing or spoken word, engage in a compassionate conversation. Address their pain, fears, and needs, and offer words of comfort and understanding. This dialogue nurtures the reintegration process.

Step 6: Ritual of Integration.

Craft a ritual that signifies the integration of your retrieved soul fragments. This could involve lighting a unity candle, creating a collage, or meditating. Infuse this ritual with your intention to honor and welcome back the lost parts of yourself.

Step 7: Artistic Expression.

Express your experience through creative outlets such as painting, writing, or dancing. Let your emotions flow onto the canvas or page, allowing your soul's journey to take form in artistic expression. This practice solidifies the sense of reclamation and transformation.

Step 8: Gratitude Ritual.

Design a ritual to express gratitude for your retrieved soul fragments. This could involve making a small offering to nature, writing a thank-you letter to yourself, or performing a kind gesture for someone else. Gratitude anchors the healing process in positivity.

Step 9: Daily Connection.

Incorporate daily rituals to maintain your connection with the retrieved aspects of your soul—practice mindfulness, meditation, or journaling to continue nurturing your sense of wholeness and integration.

Step 10: Future Empowerment.

As you move forward, carry the wisdom and strength of your retrieved soul fragments. Embrace life's challenges with newfound resilience and insight. Trust that you are now equipped to face adversity from a place of authenticity and inner power.

This Soul-relieving self-therapy offers a profound way to overcome loss trauma by tapping into the timeless wisdom of reconnecting with your soul's essence. Through these practices, you initiate a process of reclamation, integration, and empowerment. By embracing this transformative journey, you lay the foundation for a life lived authentically and harmoniously, with the strength and wisdom of your retrieved soul fragments guiding your way.

Section 4: The many forms of Violence.

As we go deeper into our inner rooms, we encounter the deeply unsettling demon of violence – a trauma that leaves profound imprints on the soul. Violence, in its multifaceted forms, disrupts the delicate equilibrium of life, casting long shadows of anguish and suffering across individuals and communities. This section invites us to step into the shadows, confront the trauma of violence directly, and explore the intricate web it weaves within the human psyche.

The roots of violent trauma are often traced back to power dynamics, unbridled aggression, and the transgression of boundaries. It emerges from the collision of vulnerability and cruelty, causing deep wounds beyond physical harm. Violence can manifest diversely – from physical abuse to emotional manipulation, from systemic oppression to domestic turmoil. These experiences shape our perceptions, intensifying emotions of fear, helplessness, and anger.

The noise of violent trauma echoes through the core of our being, rumbling in the deepest corners of our minds. It fragments our sense of safety, leaving us hyper-vigilant to potential threats. Nightmares, flashbacks, and heightened alertness become our constant companions, haunting reminders of the trauma we endured. The emotional scars are profound, often presenting as anxiety disorders, depression, or complex post-traumatic stress.

Individuals confronted with the "demon" of violence often wrestle with many consequences, some visible and others concealed. Their relationships can be deeply affected, trust shattered, and intimacy marred by fear. They might isolate themselves to escape triggers or react defensively, trapped in a cycle of emotional turmoil. Violence trauma can hinder personal growth, leaving individuals plagued by self-doubt, low self-esteem, and a sense of worthlessness.

As survivors traverse the terrain of violent trauma, a pathway to healing gradually emerges. This journey demands immense courage and self-compassion. It commences by acknowledging the pain, allowing room for grief, anger, and confusion. Engaging in trauma-informed therapy can be instrumental in uncovering layers of pain and establishing a sense of security. Cultivating mindfulness and grounding techniques empowers survivors to reconnect with the present moment, anchoring them in their healing process.

The healing journey also entails reclaiming personal agency. Survivors learn to redefine their narrative, transforming from victims to victors. This transformation involves setting boundaries, asserting one's voice, and seeking justice whenever possible. The resilience that emerges from violent trauma is a testament to the human spirit's ability to surmount adversity.

Collectively, we must confront societal structures that perpetuate violence and advocate for change. By raising awareness, supporting survivors, and fostering a culture of empathy, we can cultivate a safer world for all. Together, we can unravel the layers of violence and trauma and work towards a future where healing, empowerment, and compassion prevail.

In this section, we navigate the harsh landscape of violent trauma, acknowledging its impact and illuminating the path to healing. Through understanding, empathy, and a steadfast commitment to change, we strive to transform the legacy of violence into a gift of resilience and hope.

Section 4.1 The Marks of Violence.

Experiencing violence can have a profound and lasting effect on individuals, shaping how they think and feel in various ways. People who have gone through violent experiences might show a range of behaviors and traits that reflect the profound impact of these experiences on their mental and emotional well-being.

Hyperarousal and Hypervigilance: Individuals with the trauma of violence often experience heightened states of alertness and hypervigilance. They remain on edge, expecting danger even in seemingly safe environments. This hyperarousal can lead to difficulties in relaxation, disrupted sleep patterns, and a constant readiness to respond to perceived threats.

Emotional Dysregulation: The emotional aftermath of violence can result in intense and unpredictable emotional responses. Survivors may struggle to manage emotions such as anger, fear, and sadness, leading to emotional outbursts or numbing. This emotional dysregulation may impact their ability to engage in healthy relationships and cope with daily stressors.

Avoidance Behaviors: A hallmark of trauma, avoidance behaviors manifest as efforts to avoid reminders of the traumatic event. Individuals may avoid certain places, situations, or people associated with the violence. This avoidance can serve as a coping mechanism to prevent distressing memories from resurfacing, but it can also limit their ability to engage with life fully.

Re-experiencing and Intrusive Thoughts: Intrusive memories, nightmares, and flashbacks are common trauma symptoms. People with the trauma of violence may find themselves involuntarily reliving the traumatic event, experiencing intense emotional and physical reactions as if the event is happening in the present moment.

Social Isolation and Trust Issues: The violence trauma can erode an individual's ability to trust others and form close relationships. Survivors may withdraw from social interactions to avoid potential triggers or re-traumatization. They may struggle to create deep connections due to a heightened fear of betrayal or harm.

Survivor Guilt and Shame: Feelings of guilt and shame often accompany the trauma of violence, even when survivors are not responsible for the traumatic event. They may question whether they could have done something differently to prevent the violence or feel shame for being a victim. These emotions can lead to a negative self-perception and hinder the healing process.

Physical Symptoms: The trauma of violence can manifest in physical symptoms such as headaches, gastrointestinal issues, muscle tension, and chronic pain. These somatic symptoms arise from the intricate connection between the mind and the body, highlighting the far-reaching impact of trauma.

Substance Abuse and Self-Destructive Behavior: Some individuals with the trauma of violence may turn to substance abuse or self-destructive behaviors to cope with pain. Substance use can temporarily numb emotional distress, but it often exacerbates the long-term effects of trauma and hinders the healing process.

It's important to note that the traits and behaviors exhibited by survivors of violent trauma are complex and vary widely among individuals. While some may display these characteristics, others may cope in different ways. Addressing the trauma of violence requires a comprehensive and individualized approach, considering each person's unique experiences and needs. Healing involves creating a safe space to process the trauma, seeking professional guidance, and employing strategies to rebuild a sense of safety, trust, and self-empowerment.

Healing tool 7.5 Healing from Violence Trauma: A Self-Guided Psychotherapy Journey.

This self-guided therapy approach draws upon evidence-based techniques to guide you toward reclaiming your sense of safety, rebuilding your emotional well-being, and finding empowerment in the face of trauma.

1. **Creating a Safe Space:** Begin by setting aside dedicated time and a physical space to engage in this self-therapy practice. Ensure that you are in a comfortable environment free from distractions.
2. **Mindful Awareness:** Practice mindfulness to cultivate present-moment awareness. This involves focusing on your breath, bodily sensations, and thoughts without judgment. Mindfulness helps create a sense of groundedness and calm.
3. **Narrative Expression:** Engage in narrative expression by writing down your experiences in a journal. Allow your thoughts and feelings to flow onto the pages without censorship. This process helps externalize emotions, allowing you to process and make sense of your feelings.
4. **Safe Visualization:** Close your eyes and visualize a place or situation where you feel safe and secure. Immerse yourself in this imagery, engaging all your senses. This visualization technique can help alleviate anxiety and provide a safe mental refuge.
5. **Progressive Muscle Relaxation:** Practice progressive muscle relaxation to release physical tension. Starting from your toes and working your way up, tense and then release each

muscle group. This technique promotes relaxation and can reduce the physical impact of trauma.

6. **Positive Affirmations:** Create a list of positive affirmations that counter the negative beliefs stemming from the trauma. Repeat these affirmations daily, fostering a sense of self-worth and resilience.

7. **Gentle Exposure:** Gradually expose yourself to triggers related to the trauma in a controlled manner. Start with less distressing triggers and work your way up. This technique helps desensitize your emotional response and regain a sense of mastery.

8. **Grounding Techniques:** Practice grounding techniques when you feel overwhelmed. Focus on your immediate surroundings, identifying objects and sensations to bring yourself back to the present moment.

9. **Breathwork for Regulation:** Engage in regulated breathing exercises to manage anxiety and stress. Techniques like diaphragmatic breathing can help stabilize your nervous system and promote emotional balance.

Healing from violent trauma is an ongoing process that requires dedication and self-compassion. This self-guided psychotherapy approach integrates evidence-based techniques to empower you on your healing journey. Remember, you are not alone, and with time, effort, and the right tools, you can reclaim your sense of self and build a future defined by resilience and strength.

Healing tool 7.6 Soul Retrieving for Healing Violence Trauma: A Guided Path to Wholeness.

In the context of overcoming violent trauma, this technique becomes a profound tool for reconnecting with fragmented parts of our being and reclaiming our sense of wholeness. This self-guided Soul Retrieving journey draws from traditional wisdom and modern therapeutic insights to guide you toward healing and transformation.

1. **Creating a Sacred Space:** Create a physical and mental space that feels sacred and safe. Find a quiet corner where you won't be disturbed and gather objects that hold meaning.

2. **Breath and Centering:** Practice deep breathing to center yourself. Inhale slowly, feel the breath fill your lungs, and exhale, releasing tension. Allow your breath to become a rhythmic anchor for your journey.

3. **Connecting with Your Inner Sanctuary:** Close your eyes and visualize a serene inner sanctuary—a place of refuge within yourself. Imagine this space vividly, incorporating sounds, scents, and textures that invoke feelings of safety.

4. **Meeting Your Inner Guide:** In your inner sanctuary, invite an inner guide—a symbol of wisdom and compassion. This could be an animal, a spiritual figure, or any representation that resonates with you.

5. **Journey to the Wounded Self:** With your inner guide by your side, embark on a gentle journey into the depths of your psyche. Visualize yourself approaching a wounded aspect of yourself, representing the trauma of violence.

6. **Engage in Compassionate Dialogue:** Initiate a compassionate dialogue with this wounded aspect. Ask questions like, "What do you need?", "What messages do you hold?" and "How can I help you heal?"

7. **Integration and Healing:** As you engage in this dialogue, offer support, understanding, and love to the wounded aspect. Listen attentively to its responses and offer reassurance that you are here to facilitate healing.

8. **Reclaiming and Integrating:** Imagine extending your hand to the wounded aspect, inviting it to reintegrate with your being. Feel the fusion of this aspect, once fragmented, back into your core self. Experience a sense of completeness.

9. **Anchoring the Healing:** Before concluding your Soul Retrieving journey, visualize a radiant light surrounding your

integrated self. This light represents healing, protection, and transformation.

10. **Gratitude and Closure:** Express gratitude to your inner guide for its guidance and support. Slowly bring your awareness back to the present moment, feeling grounded and whole.

Soul Retrieving offers a powerful pathway to healing violent trauma, allowing you to reconnect with parts of yourself that may have been lost or suppressed. You can embark on a journey toward wholeness and transformation through compassionate dialogue, integration, and guidance of your inner sanctuary and guide. Remember, this practice is deeply personal, and each step is an invitation to embrace healing with love, courage, and resilience.

Section 4: Unveiling the Multifaceted Spectrum of Trauma: A Path to Wholeness.

Within our inner world, trauma wears different faces, each imprinting its mark on our minds and coloring our view of the world. We've explored fundamental traumas like neglect, abuse, loss, and violence. Now, let's unravel the subtle yet impactful traumas woven into our inner lives' fabric.

Betrayal trauma, arising from shattered trust in close relationships, shares a common thread with the trauma of abuse. Both erode the foundation of security we hold in our connections, leaving behind emotional scars that can take years to heal. Similarly, identity trauma and shame trauma echo the themes of neglect, as they are rooted in the denial of our authentic selves and the feeling of unworthiness. Discrimination trauma, stemming from external prejudice, bears semblance to violence trauma in that both involve the harm inflicted upon us by external forces.

The beauty of our journey lies in the tools we've amassed, the lanterns guiding us through the darkness. The nurturing of our inner child, born from the wellspring of self-compassion, doesn't just apply to neglect trauma; it cradles us through the thorns of betrayal and discrimination, offering solace to wounds that echo through our identity. Our journey toward reclaiming purpose, intertwined with healing from loss trauma, also extends its hand to help us unearth our authentic identity, fractured by betrayal and discrimination.

The array of empathy and self-awareness we've woven to address abuse trauma finds its purpose in shame and identity trauma. Just as we've learned to dismantle the chains of violent trauma with forgiveness and self-empowerment, these tools illuminate the path toward freeing ourselves from the bondage of shame and the shadows of an identity crisis. Our toolbox is comprehensive and all-encompassing.

Our healing, rooted in the excavation of our inner house, ripples across traumas, harmonizing the discordant notes into a symphony of resilience. As we venture into the chapters that lie ahead, let us remember that the power of healing is not confined to one demon alone; it is an echo that reverberates through the corridors of our being, transforming darkness into light, pain into growth, and trauma into strength.

CHAPTER 8: BREAKING THE CHAINS OF GENERATIONAL TRAUMA - LIBERATION AND EMPOWERMENT

The effects of generational trauma run deep in our lives, stemming from the stories of our ancestors. It shapes our experiences, perceptions, and even our biology. In this chapter, we aim to untangle ourselves from the chains of the past and seek healing for ourselves, those who came before us, and those who will come after us.

The Legacy of Inherited Pain: Generational trauma is an inheritance of suffering passed down through the generations like a silent whisper. It originates in historical injustices, unresolved grief, and unhealed wounds that stretch far beyond our lifetimes. Once unspoken and unseen, the pain of our ancestors takes residence within us, coloring our perceptions and influencing our choices. The never-fully acknowledged trauma becomes a heavy mantle we unknowingly carry.

The Echoes in Our Lives: These ancestral echoes manifest in myriad ways. The patterns of self-sabotage, the unexplained fears, and the relationships that mirror past dynamics—are all footprints of generational trauma. Just as our past trauma can hold us hostage, so can the unresolved pain of those who came before us. The cycle continues until we summon the courage to break free from its grasp and rewrite our narrative.

Healing Through Ancestral Empowerment: Liberating ourselves from generational trauma is not just an act of personal healing; it's a profound act of honoring our lineage and creating a brighter future. By delving into the stories of our ancestors, acknowledging their pain, and extending compassion to them, we initiate a process of healing that transcends time. We realize that we are healing for ourselves and those who could not find their healing.

Reclaiming Our Power: The path to breaking the chains of generational trauma involves a journey of self-discovery, self-compassion, and resilience. Through guided practices, we learn to identify the inherited patterns that have held us back and develop tools to transform them into sources of strength. By healing ourselves, we disrupt the cycle of pain, empowering ourselves to make choices that align with our true desires and potential.

Healing as a Ripple Effect: As we free ourselves from the shackles of generational trauma, we become beacons of transformation for our lineage. The healing that starts within us radiates outward, influencing the collective consciousness of our family, community, and beyond. Our recovery catalyzes generational healing, sparking a ripple effect that touches lives across time and space.

A Call to Transcendence: In our journey to break the chains of generational trauma, we are called to transcend the limitations of our past. We embrace the power to rewrite the story, to transform pain into purpose, and to create a legacy of resilience and empowerment. As we embark on this path, remember that we are not alone. We stand as a link between the past and the future, and in our healing, we hold the potential to shape a brighter, liberated world for ourselves and generations to come.

Activity 8.1: Exploring Your Generational Legacy.

Instructions:

1. **Create a Generational Timeline:** Create a timeline of your family's history. List major events, milestones, and significant experiences from at least three generations back. This could include birthdates, marriages, migrations, wars, immigrations, divorces, deaths, and other notable occurrences.
2. **Identify Patterns:** Review the timeline and look for repeated patterns across generations. These patterns could be related to relationships, career choices, mental health, physical health, substance use, financial challenges, or other aspects.
3. **Reflect on Family Stories:** Think about the stories you've heard from your parents, grandparents, and relatives. Are there any recurring themes or narratives? Consider whether there are any unspoken rules or taboos in your family that might indicate hidden trauma.
4. **Explore Unexplained Emotions:** Reflect on your emotional reactions and triggers. Are there emotions that seem out of proportion to the current situation? Explore whether these emotions might be connected to generational trauma.
5. **Interview Family Members:** Reach out to family members and discuss the family's history and experiences. Ask open-ended questions to encourage them to share their perspectives and memories.
6. **Ancestral Connections:** Spend time in quiet reflection or meditation. Imagine connecting with your ancestors and asking them to reveal any unresolved issues or traumas they might have carried. Allow your intuition to guide you.

7. **Physical Manifestations:** Consider any chronic health issues, physical symptoms, or conditions that seem to run in your family. Explore whether these might be linked to generational trauma.

8. **Expressive Arts:** Use art, writing, or other creative outlets to explore your family's history and the emotions surrounding it. Expressing yourself creatively can often reveal hidden insights.

9. **Journaling Prompts:** Write about how the patterns and events from your family history might have influenced your beliefs, behaviors, and experiences. Consider how these patterns might be connected to generational trauma.

Remember, this activity is about gentle exploration and understanding. Uncovering generational trauma can be a transformative journey, leading to greater self-awareness and healing. Be patient and honor your emotions as you delve into this process.

Section 1: Comprehensive Generational Trauma Healing and Liberation through Soul Retrieving.

Generational trauma weaves a complex multi-soul connection that spans time, impacting our present selves, ancestors, and future generations. Utilizing the profound technique of Soul Retrieving, we embark on a transformative journey of healing, liberation, and empowerment that spans time.

Phase 1: Connecting with Ancestral Wisdom

1. **Ancestral Meditation:** Begin by creating a sacred space and practice deep meditation. Visualize a bridge connecting you with your ancestors. With each breath, imagine traversing this bridge, entering their realm, and inviting them to share their wisdom.

2. **Ancestral Dialogue:** Engage in a soul conversation with your ancestors. Seek their guidance, ask about their experiences, and invite them to share their challenges and triumphs. Listen closely to their messages, for they hold the keys to understanding the roots of generational trauma.

Phase 2: Soul Retrieving for Self.

1. **Recalling Fragmented Aspects:** Through Soul Retrieving, journey within yourself to retrieve fragmented aspects of your soul that hold the imprints of generational trauma. With intention, gather these aspects and welcome them back into your being.
2. **Healing and Integration:** Create a sacred space to communicate with these retrieved aspects. Engage in the process of healing, compassionately addressing their pain and wounds. Visualize them integrating into your present self, infusing you with strength and resilience.

Phase 3: Liberating Ancestral Trauma.

1. **Offering Ceremony:** In a meditative state, hold an offering ceremony for your ancestors. Express your intention to heal and liberate their pain. Imagine offering them love, light, and your willingness to carry forward their legacy of healing.
2. **Transmutation Ritual:** Visualize a portal of light where ancestral pain can be transmuted. Channel healing energy towards this portal, imagining it is releasing the burdens of trauma. Witness as the energy transforms into healing light that envelops your ancestors.

Phase 4: Blessing Future Generations.

1. **Soul Retrieving for Future Generations:** Extend the Soul Retrieving technique to future generations. Journey into the realm of potential and retrieve the souls of your descendants. Embrace them with love, wisdom, and a commitment to break the chains of generational trauma.
2. **Blessing Ceremony:** In a meditative state, hold a blessing ceremony for your future generations. Envision them bathed in a radiant light of healing and empowerment. Affirm their resilience and their capacity to thrive unburdened by the trauma of the past.

Phase 5: Creating an Ancestral Healing Sanctuary.

1. **Sacred Space Dedication:** Dedicate a physical space to your ancestors. Create an altar adorned with symbols, photos, and offerings that honor their presence. This space is a focal point for your ongoing connection and healing work.
2. **Regular Connection:** Visit your ancestral sanctuary regularly. Engage in meditation, prayer, or rituals to maintain the connection with your ancestors and continue the healing process.

By embarking on this comprehensive journey of Soul Retrieving, you weave a harmonious bond between your past, present, and future. The retrieved aspects of your soul healed ancestral pain, and the blessings bestowed upon future generations intertwine to create a symphony of transformation. As you traverse the dimensions of time, remember that the healing you initiate within yourself radiates outwards, touching the lives of your ancestors and sculpting a legacy of resilience and liberation for generations to come.

CHAPTER 9: CONCLUSION.

As we conclude this transformative journey through the chapters of *Coffee with My Demons Part 2: The Past*, we find ourselves at the threshold of profound healing and self-discovery. The path we've walked together has led us through the intricate labyrinth of our inner house, where we encountered inner "demons" born from neglect, abuse, loss, violence, and the legacy of generational trauma. Each step we took was an act of courage, a declaration of our commitment to break free from the chains that bound us.

In the utmost human existence, we have explored the depths of our pain, confronting the shadows that long sought to hold us captive. Through the power of soul retrieval, memory healing, and proven psychotherapy techniques, we unearthed the layers of these "demons," recognizing how they manifested and impacted our lives. We unveiled the roots of insecurity, the wounds of neglect, the scars of abuse, the echoes of loss, and the echoes of violence.

In this journey, we've come face to face with the most formidable of adversaries—our past. With unwavering determination, we navigated the stormy waters of trauma, learning that the path to liberation is not always linear or without its challenges. Yet, we persevered, armed with the tools of self-compassion, introspection, and resilience.

As we close this chapter, let us reflect on the significance of our collective efforts. We have engaged in deep introspection, meditation, and self-therapy, unearthing wounds buried deep within. In the process, we uncovered the interconnectedness of our experiences—how the trauma of one generation can cast its shadow across the next. We shattered the illusion that we are isolated beings, understanding that our stories are woven into the fabric of our ancestry.

By healing ourselves, we extend healing to our ancestors and offer a brighter future to future generations. Our journey is not just about our liberation; it's a courageous act of breaking the cycle, rewriting the narrative, and reclaiming the essence of our true selves. In embracing our pain, we transcend its grip, transforming it into a source of wisdom and strength.

Let this be the chapter of closure, not just for the "demons" we've faced, but for the parts of ourselves that we've neglected. Let it be the prelude to a new narrative, one that is marked by empowerment, authenticity, and self-love. Armed with the lessons learned from our past, we step into the future with newfound clarity, resilience, and an unshakable sense of worthiness.

Remember that healing is a continuous journey as the curtain falls on this volume. The tools and techniques we've explored here are not just confined to these pages; they are seeds you can carry into your daily life, nurturing them as they bloom into transformative practices. Let them guide you through the currents of your emotions, the echoes of your memories, and the tapestry of your existence.

May you continue to walk this path with strength and grace. May you cultivate the self-compassion that nourishes your soul, the introspection that unveils your truth, and the resilience that propels you forward. As you savor your coffee with these demons, may it be a testament to your courage, growth, and unwavering commitment to becoming your best self.

With gratitude for joining us on this journey, we bid farewell to this volume, knowing that our paths may cross again as we explore the depths of our souls. Until then, remember that the pages of this book are not an end but a beginning—a beginning of the liberation that comes from embracing every facet of who you are.

CHAPTER 10: CELEBRATING YOUR JOURNEY.

Congratulations, dear reader, for completing the transformative journey through *Coffee with My Demons Part 2: The Past.* Your commitment to self-discovery, healing, and growth has led you to a moment of empowerment, clarity, and renewed purpose.

As you close this volume, take a moment to reflect on the distance you've traveled. You've delved deep into the recesses of your inner house, bravely facing the "demons" that once held you captive. Your willingness to confront the past, to heal the wounds, and to embrace the lessons learned is a testament to your strength and resilience.

Remember, this journey is not just about acknowledging the pain—it's about transforming it into a wellspring of wisdom and strength. As you carry the insights and tools gained from these pages, know that you can create positive change in your life and the lives of those around you.

With your strides through the realm of the past, you stand at the threshold of a new dawn—a future with boundless potential, purpose, and joy. As you gaze toward *Coffee with My Demons Part 3: The Future,* prepare to embark on an exhilarating and transformative discovery voyage.

In this upcoming volume, we will journey beyond the echoes of past struggles, transcending the confines of the present moment and stepping boldly into the uncharted landscape of the future. Together, we will explore pathways to finding your purpose, cultivating constant happiness, reshaping your outlook on life, and fully unleashing your innate potential.

Imagine a life where you navigate each day with a renewed sense of purpose, where happiness becomes your constant companion, and where yesterday's setbacks fuel today's determination. In *Part 3: The Future*, we will navigate the terrains of self-discovery, personal growth, and authentic expression, equipping you with the tools to navigate the complexities of modern existence with resilience and grace.

As we look ahead to this next chapter of your journey, know that the past has laid the foundation for the remarkable transformation that awaits you. Your dedication to self-improvement and your unwavering commitment to your well-being are the driving forces that will carry you forward.

Prepare to embrace a life brimming with purpose, happiness, and fulfillment. The journey continues, and the future beckons. Get ready to embark on this extraordinary expedition—one that will lead you to the abundant, vibrant, and limitless future you deserve.

"THIS IS THE BOOK I WISH YOU WOULD HAVE READ"

BONUS CHAPTER: WAITING FOR THE NEXT SIP.

As we bring this journey through "Coffee with My Demons Part 2: The Past" to a temporary pause, it's natural to wonder what to do. The space between volumes can be a unique opportunity to reflect, integrate, and prepare for the next leg of your inner exploration. While awaiting the arrival of "Coffee with My Demons Part 3: The Future," there are several meaningful tasks and practices you can engage in to continue your progress and maintain your momentum.

1. Revisit and Reflect:

• Take time to revisit the self-therapy exercises and insights from both Part 1 and Part 2. Reflect on your progress, the lessons learned, and the changes you've experienced.

2. Journal Your Journey:

• Keep a journal to document your thoughts, emotions, and revelations as you process the material from the first two parts. Writing can be a powerful tool for self-discovery and growth.

3. Deepen Self-Care Practices:

- Build upon the self-care routines you've cultivated in Part 1 and Part 2. Whether meditation, physical exercise, or creative outlets, invest in activities that nurture your well-being.

4. Expand Your Reading List:

- Explore books, articles, and resources that align with inner growth, self-discovery, and healing themes. This can broaden your perspective and introduce new insights.

5. Engage in Mindfulness:

- Practice mindfulness in your daily life. Please consider your thoughts, feelings, and experiences as they arise, cultivating present-moment awareness.

6. Connect with Support:

- Maintain connections with any support networks you've established during your journey. Share your progress, challenges, and aspirations with trusted friends or a support group.

7. Set Intentions for Part 3:

- Take this time to set intentions for "Coffee with My Demons Part 3: The Future." Reflect on what you hope to gain from the next volume and how you envision your journey unfolding.

8. Explore New Interests:

- Use the interim period to explore new hobbies or interests. Engaging in activities you enjoy can foster a sense of fulfillment and joy.

9. Practice Gratitude:

- Cultivate gratitude for the progress you've made so far. Recognize the strength and resilience you've demonstrated in facing your inner demons.

10. Embrace Patience: - Remember that healing and growth are ongoing processes. Embrace patience as you await the arrival of Part 3 and continue to navigate your journey.

As you engage in these practices and tasks, remember that your journey toward self-discovery and healing is ongoing. Each step you take, whether during the chapters of "Coffee with My Demons Part 1 and 2" or the anticipation of Part 3, contributes to your overall transformation. With a heart full of courage and an openness to change, you're well on your way to embracing a future that promises fulfillment, purpose, and a deeper understanding of yourself. Stay committed, curious, and sipping that transformative coffee of self-awareness and empowerment.

SPECIAL NOTE:

Dear Readers,

As I pen these final words, I'm filled with profound gratitude for your unwavering commitment to your journey of self-discovery and healing. Our collective voyage through the pages of "Coffee with My Demons Part 2: The Past" has been a profound exploration of the human experience—a tapestry woven with shadows and light, struggles and triumphs.

As you prepare to embrace the horizon of "Coffee with My Demons Part 3: The Future," remember that your path is a testament to your resilience, courage, and unwavering determination. The metaphorical demons we've encountered together are not adversaries to be defeated but mirrors reflecting the profound potential within you. Each step you take is a testament to your willingness to confront discomfort, embrace vulnerability, and emerge stronger on the other side.

The journey within is a lifelong odyssey that holds the key to unlocking the treasures of your authentic self. In the depths of your experiences, you've unearthed wisdom and insights that can illuminate your path. While we may carry the scars of the past, we also hold the capacity to heal, grow, and redefine our narratives.

As we part ways for now, let these words resonate within you: You are not defined by your past, nor are you bound by the limitations of your inner "demons." You possess an innate resilience that has carried you through moments of darkness and propelled you toward moments of illumination. Your journey is a sacred dance—a rhythm that intertwines moments of chaos and clarity, despair and hope, uncertainty and empowerment.

May the lessons you've gleaned from the pages of this book serve as lanterns to guide you as you navigate the uncharted waters of your future. Trust in your ability to cultivate self-love, embrace change, and harness the power of your inner potential. With every sip of the transformative coffee of self-awareness, you inch closer to embodying the fullest expression of yourself.

In the quiet moments when doubt may attempt to creep in, remember the strength you've summoned thus far. The road ahead may be winding, but it's paved with growth, purpose, and the boundless capacity for love and joy. You possess the tools, the resilience, and the inner fire to transcend perceived limitations and flourish in embracing your authenticity.

As we prepare to unveil the next volume of "Coffee with My Demons Part 3: The Future," know that your journey is far from over—it's a perpetual evolution, an ongoing narrative that you are both the author and protagonist of. Embrace the infinite possibilities that lie ahead, for your journey is one of self-discovery, transformation, and the unwavering pursuit of a life lived in full color.

With heartfelt gratitude and anticipation for what lies ahead,

Dr. Alec Laracuente

BIBLIOGRAPHY.

Psychotherapy:

1. Johnson, S. M. (2019). Attachment theory in practice: Emotionally focused therapy (EFT) with individuals, couples, and families—the Guilford Press.
2. Hayes, S. C., Strosahl, K. D., & Wilson, K. G. (2012). Acceptance and commitment therapy: The process and practice of mindful change. Guilford Press.
3. Linehan, M. M. (2015). DBT skills training manual. Guilford Publications.
4. Yalom, I. D. (2002). The gift of therapy: An open letter to a new generation of therapists and their patients. HarperCollins.

Soul Retrieval and Healing:

1. Ingerman, S. (1991). Soul retrieval: Mending the fragmented self. HarperOne.
2. Villoldo, A. (2014). Healing the Luminous Body: The Way of the Shaman. Sounds True.
3. Myss, C. M. (1997). Anatomy of the spirit: The seven stages of power and healing. Harmony.
4. Moss, R. (2010). The secret history of dreaming. New World Library.
5. Wesselman, H. (2013). The Journey to the Sacred Garden: A Guide to Traveling in the Spiritual Realms. Hay House.

www.ingramcontent.com/pod-product-compliance
Lightning Source LLC
Chambersburg PA
CBHW060504130626
46553CB00002B/404